# Black

# Swan

# Blues

## By Paul Slade

*Black Swan Blues*

ISBN: 978-1-5272-9697-8

Contact:

paul@planetslade.com

This expanded 2021 edition marks the 100th anniversary of Harry Pace founding Black Swan.

*Black Swan Blues*

For my parents.


"Almapa"

*Black Swan Blues*

# Table of contents

*Black Swan Blues*

# Introduction

Forty years before Motown there was Black Swan.

All but forgotten now, this pioneering blues label was the first successful Black-owned record company in America. Until Harry Pace launched Black Swan in 1921, the white-owned labels' monopoly had been broken only by Broome Records, a tiny regional operation which managed to release fewer than a dozen sides before it collapsed. Black Swan racked up nearly 30 times that total, releasing around 350 tracks before it was done. It was not until Vee-Jay reached its third birthday in 1956 that another Black-owned label hit those numbers, and not until Motown hit its 1960s peak that one matched Black Swan's impact on American life.

Like Motown's Berry Gordy, Pace was a young Black American songwriter who grew angry at the way white moguls were treating his community's music. Like Gordy, he began by recording only Black artists, promoted his label with a nationwide revue tour and soon found white people were buying the records too. Like Motown, Black Swan created many new stars, only to find them poached by richer white-owned rivals. And, like Motown, Black Swan formed a crucial link in the chain that later gave us The Beatles and The Rolling Stones.

The difference is that Pace achieved all this in an era when Black businessmen and performers faced a level of racist persecution which Gordy's artists could barely imagine. The Motown troupe had shots fired above their heads in Alabama, yes, but that pales beside the 1922 incident when the body of a lynched young Black man was flung into a Macon theatre's lobby

1

shortly before it hosted a Black Swan show. Pace's white rivals were determined to undermine the label at every turn, from sabotaging his manufacturing plans to blocking his distribution to poaching his stars with a series of dirty tricks. Fortunately, he was up to the challenge.

Pace was a dapper, well-educated, refined young man, who got his start in the music business through a chance meeting with the legendary WC Handy in Memphis. After a brief spell writing songs together, the two men set up the music publishing company Pace & Handy, where Pace's business genius ensured Handy tunes like *St Louis Blues* became big earners. A couple of years running a small Black magazine for WEB DuBois had given Pace a formidable network of business contacts, which he built on further with a parallel career in banking and insurance as he licked Pace & Handy into shape. When the time came to make his leap from printed sheet music sales to the exciting new technology of phonograph discs, he was more than ready.

The few record labels that existed in 1921 were all white-owned and allowed Black singers to record only the demeaning "coon" songs of the minstrel shows. It was the feisty white-owned Okeh Records which first broke that embargo with Mamie Smith's *Crazy Blues* – now recognized as the first genuine blues disc of all – but Pace was hot on its heels. His Black Swan release of Ethel Waters singing *Down Home Blues* sold well over 100,000 copies – enough for a massive hit in those days – and prompted every white-owned label to start recording Black blues singers too.

Without the push provided by Black Swan's success, the major labels may have delayed their own acceptance of Black artists by a year or more. That doesn't sound like much to make a fuss about, but it would have taken a delay of only 21 months for Robert Johnson to have died without recording a note - and it was records like Johnson's which first inspired John Lennon and Keith Richards to pick up a guitar.

Ethel Waters got her start at Black Swan and is now recognized as the template for a whole school of jazz singers who followed her: Billie Holiday, Ella Fitzgerald, Sarah Vaughan. Lena Horne called Waters "the mother of us all". Fletcher Henderson started his career at Black Swan too, learning his blues chops there, meeting Louis Armstrong for the first time on a Black Swan tour, and feeding all that experience into his invention of swing music 15 years later. Remove those two bricks from popular music's foundations, and the whole structure begins to take a different shape.

This is the story of a remarkable record label and of Harry Pace, the even more remarkable man who founded it.

**A note on language:** Most of this book takes place between 1900 and 1940, when the language used to discuss race was very different from our own. African-American writers like DuBois, Handy and Pace routinely used terms like "Negro", "colored" and "the race" to discuss their community, employing them as simple descriptive words with no connotation of offence. Pace regularly used all these terms in his own ads and packaging – something he'd never have done if his Black customer base viewed them with any distaste.

# Exceptional men

*"To those whose sensibilities were easily offended Beale Street was repulsive. To one who was squeamish it was shocking. But to one who could plumb the depths of human emotions, Beale Street had a never-ending interest, for here were found all the frailties and weaknesses of humanity. Here every appetite was pandered to, and every human impulse was quickened."*
**- Harry Pace in his 1934 novel *Memphis Blues*.**

As the twentieth century got underway, Beale Street in Memphis was one of the liveliest centres of Black life anywhere in America. Abandoned by the city's white elite in the yellow fever outbreaks of the 1870s, this eight-block stretch of packed real estate leading to the Mississippi River now hosted a string of saloons, dancehalls, gambling joints and brothels which throbbed with jazz and ragtime music every night. The riverboats docking nearby provided a constant stream of thirsty travellers and dockhands, all of whom knew – as one appalled hellfire preacher had put it – that you could get drunk quicker on Beale than anywhere else in the city.

Battier's Drug Store, handily located on the corner of what's now BB King Boulevard, served as Beale Street's emergency room, patching up each night's injuries from bar fights and drunken shootings. Just a few doors away was Pee Wee's Saloon, a favourite hangout for WC Handy and many of the city's other leading Black musicians. Handy, who lived nearby, would later list the street's charms in his landmark 1917 song *Beale Street Blues*, mentioning its finely-dressed dandies, its pickpockets, thugs, drunks, straying husbands and bums. "I'd rather be there than any place I know," he happily concludes.

So little sway did whites have over Beale Street in those days that the Jim Crow laws ruling life elsewhere in the South could be forgotten, allowing Black customers and musicians to walk in the front door of their chosen establishment rather than being directed to the demeaning tradesmen's entrance out back. For the African-Americans of this era, a thousand petty indignities dropped away the moment they set foot on Beale, and that made it a magnet for the brightest, most talented and most entrepreneurial people the Black South had to offer. None were sharper – or more successful - than Robert Church.

Church was a very savvy Black businessman who'd bought up a lot of Memphis property cheap during the city's various run-ins with yellow fever - a series of deals which eventually made him the South's first Black millionaire. By 1900 he was Beale Street's acknowledged king and using the profits provided by his establishments there to to fund a range of philanthropic projects like the building of Church Park. In 1906, he founded Solvent Savings Bank to provide loans for the Black entrepreneurs and would-be homeowners who the white banks routinely turned away. Solvent's HQ was right there on Beale Street, and when the bank found itself with liquidity problems in 1907, the man it called on to sort them out was Harry Pace.

\*\*\*

Most of what we know about Pace's background comes from a 1917 profile in the Georgia edition of Arthur Caldwell's *History of the American Negro* series. Then just 33 years old and with all his major achievements still in front of him, Pace was already being marked out as a man of extraordinary ability and someone who Caldwell felt merited a full three pages in his book.

Like many of the other Black achievers profiled there, Pace had started from nothing. "His grandfather was brought from Virginia to Georgia during the days of slavery but was manumitted by his master to whom he was related, and was made manager and overseer of the plantation," Caldwell writes. He's too discreet to spell things out any further, but the implication is clear enough: Pace's white great-grandfather had raped one of his female slaves and produced a son by her who he never fully acknowledged as his own. The most he was prepared to do was give the lad his freedom – that's what "manumitted' means - and see to it that he got a tolerable job in the plantation's hierarchy. [1, 2]

Harry's freed grandfather then had a son of his own called Charles Pace, who later became a blacksmith and lived with his wife Nancy in the rural Georgia settlement of Covington. It was there, on January 6, 1884, that Nancy gave birth to a boy who they named Harry Herbert Pace, his great-grandfather's legacy still visible in the baby's very fair skin. "His parents passed away while the boy was still young," Caldwell adds – though exactly how young remains unclear. [3]

As an adult, Pace would occasionally dabble in writing fiction, often giving his central characters a similar background to his own and driving the plot along through their sense of resentment towards the white ancestors who'd abandoned them. It's hard not to view these characters as literary stand-ins for Pace himself, who uses them to vent the strong feelings he was too disciplined to indulge in real life. Taken together, they offer one of the few clues we have about his inner world.

In his 1913 short story, *The Man Who Won*, for example, Pace's protagonist is an intelligent and educated young Black man called Russell Stanley, out for revenge on the powerful white Southerner who'd impregnated his Black mother and left her and the baby to fend for themselves. Stanley, we're told, has "pale skin and brown half-curling hair together with [a] general air of culture and refinement" – a description which, by the time he wrote this story, matched Pace himself in very detail. [4]

The same urge for revenge surfaces in his 1934 novel *Memphis Blues*. Here, one of the main characters is Cam Bright, a formidable Black gangster/entrepreneur who was fathered and abandoned by a white plantation owner. The novel's period setting places Cam in the same generation as Pace's grandfather and gives him much the same history. "[The plantation owner] had beaten him, his own son and slave, on the Mississippi plantation where he had been raised, and had sold Cam's mother down the river into the worst of plantation slavery when she dared to raise her voice in protest against his cruelty," Pace writes. "Through all these years he had held this bitterness, this desire for revenge against those of his own blood who had cheated him out of the heritage and the life that properly belonged to him". [5, 6]

Perhaps the best way to view these fictions is as a release valve for Pace's own emotions. Whatever portion of Stanley and Bright's rage Pace felt for himself, he was far too canny to let it show, but there's no denying its role as fuel for his fiction. The bloody deaths he gives to the characters representing himself in the stories – shot or hanged by white racists – reflects his conviction that open rage like theirs could only end in tragedy.

We don't know who raised Pace after he was orphaned, but it's clear he completed both his elementary and high school education, proving to his teachers in the process that they had an unusually bright child on their hands. Atlanta University, the first institution to offer African-Americans a degree-level education, gave him a place somewhere around 1900, where he studied for a Bachelor of Arts degree. His greatest good fortune there was to be mentored by Professor WEB DuBois, the great Black intellectual and writer, who lectured in sociology at the university. DuBois took Pace under his wing, encouraging him to continue developing his mind and introducing the young man to all the new worlds a university education could open up. Pace was an avid pupil. "He developed a taste for the best literature, his preference running to American and French history, and to American and English fiction and biography," says Caldwell.

Pace had taught himself the rudiments of the print trade before embarking on his degree course and hoped to pay his way through college with a job in the university's print shop. This went well until he discovered that his white colleagues there were being paid 30 cents an hour for exactly the same job he was doing, while Pace and the other Black workers got only a quarter of that rate. He walked out in protest, earning his keep with janitorial work and other menial jobs until the print shop's bosses agreed to take him back at the higher rate. He also served as editor of the college paper – presumably an unpaid role – and worked closely with DuBois in compiling material for the professor's various academic papers and other work. One of his biggest projects there was an early survey of America's Black entrepreneurs and the businesses they'd created.

Pace's time at Atlanta coincided with DuBois' work developing his ideas on how Black Americans could best improve their lot. In September 1903 – the same year Pace graduated – DuBois published these thoughts in an essay which he called *The Talented Tenth*. His argument was that any persecuted group's hopes of advancing in American society must rely on pouring resources into the education of its most gifted children. Here's an extract:

> *"The Negro race, like all races, is going to be saved by its exceptional men. Can the masses of the Negro people be in any possible way more quickly raised than by the effort and example of this aristocracy of talent and character? Was there ever a nation on God's earth civilized from the bottom upward? Never; it is, ever was and ever will be from the top downward that culture filters. The Talented Tenth rises and pull all that are worth the saving up to their vantage ground. [...] The Talented Tenth of the Negro race must be made leaders of thought and missionaries of culture among their people. No others can do this work and Negro colleges must train men for it." [7]*

You couldn't ask for a better indication of DuBois' hopes for his young protégée at Atlanta, or of his lifelong influence on Pace's thinking and the paths he'd later choose. The two men remained friends for decades to come, their companionship rooted in the father/son relationship they'd forged together at the university and the philosophy Pace absorbed there. Ideas crystallized in *The Talented Tenth* would guide his life for decades to come.

Pace was 19 when he graduated from Atlanta in 1903 as valedictorian of his class. His hope even then was to qualify as a lawyer, but he lacked the funds for further study and so took a job teaching science at the Haines

Institute in Augusta instead. His plan was to eventually save enough money from his salary there to enter Columbia University's law school in New York.

# Man on the *Moon*

*"As soon as the cloud of debts and expenses commenced to gather, DuBois and Ed Simon withdrew further financial assistance and left Pace alone to struggle with the venture. He spent everything he had to meet the expenses of getting out the magazine. Soon, he found himself penniless, his last suit of clothes threadbare and hunger almost his daily lot."*

**- Merah Stuart in his 1940 essay *An Economic Detour*.**

In March 1904, DuBois went into partnership with Edward Simon, another former student of his, to run a jobbing print shop at 358 Beale Street in Memphis. Simon had previously been working as a printing instructor at the city's LeMoyne Institute, and so had all the technical skills this new enterprise required. Funding the venture from their own pockets, DuBois and Simon kitted out the shop with nearly $2,000 worth of new machinery, earning about half that sum back in the shop's first year. Memphis then had a Black population of just under 50,000 – the fourth largest in any American city – and, with only one other Black-owned print shop in town, DuBois hoped Ed L Simon & Co would eventually become the cash cow he needed to fund a magazine of his own.

*Moon Illustrated Weekly*, he announced, would be

"a high-class journal to circulate among the intelligent Negroes, tell them of the deeds of themselves and their neighbors, interpret the news of the world to them, and inspire them towards definite ideals". Looking for a masthead slogan to sum up these ambitions, he settled on "A Record of the Darker Races". With physical distribution in Memphis and Atlanta plus subscriptions by mail to the rest of the US, he hoped to build its circulation to 100,000 copies per week. DuBois would be the magazine's editor-in-chief, and Simon would look after printing it at the Beale Street shop. All they needed now was a business manager to sell ads and oversee the *Moon's* finances. [1]

DuBois decided to offer the job to Pace, writing to him at the Haines Institute to set out what was involved. "If you could come to us on a modest salary, we could offer work as an outside man drumming up jobs for the office and work at typesetting," he explained. "When [the magazine starts], we could make you assistant in both the business and the editorial ends of that work. And, finally, if the enterprise gets on a good financial footing, we could give you a position to your liking at as good a salary as we could afford to pay." [2]

The letter closed by suggesting Pace come to Memphis so he could look over the print shop's new kit for himself and meet Simon. That trip must have gone well, because by the end of 1905, he'd quit his teaching' job to join the *Moon* full-time. Pooling their savings, the three men scraped together just enough to get the magazine started, publishing its first issue in December of that year. [3]

DuBois remained in Atlanta, contributing regular articles to the *Moon* but leaving its Memphis production work to Pace and Simon alone. Pace's main job at this time was to introduce himself to all the city's leading Black businessmen and charm as many of them as he could into buying an ad. Not everyone obliged, but even those who turned him away couldn't help but be impressed by Pace's energy and demeanor. Among the advertisers he brought in were Thomas Hayes, who owned the city's biggest Black funeral parlour ("Finest funeral cars of any colored man in the South") and the Gillis Brothers grocery chain. The city had several white-owned businesses who needed more Black customers too, and Pace's fair skin often opened doors for him there. That's how he sold *Moon* ads to Guardian Real Estate ("Lots for Good Colored People Only") and Union Painless Dentist ("Special Reductions for Colored People"). [4]

Pace's work at the *Moon* gave him a chance to meet everyone who mattered in Memphis's emerging Black middle class, and the contacts he made among them paved the way for much of his later success. As a day-to-day proposition, though, the job was a pretty miserable one. The magazine's shoestring funding meant its production standards could never match DuBois' hopes, and sales languished at around the 250-300 mark. In April 1905, DuBois wrote to a wealthy banker called Jacob Schiff, asking him to lend the magazine $10,000 to improve its appearance. "The samples are far below my ideal – the best possible on the present small capital," he confessed. In a similar letter to Isaac Seligman – this one asking for $5,000 – he admitted that "the mechanical make-up is poor and the general appearance a little slovenly".

Lack of funds was not the only problem, as Paul Partington explains in his 1986 history of the *Moon*. "DuBois in 1906 was too overly involved in a host of activities to give time to editing a magazine," he writes. "This is evidenced by numerous lectures and speeches through the North, a trip to England in August, the annual meeting of the Niagara Movement in September and a survey for the US Department of Labor in Lowndes

County, Alabama, which he did in the late Fall. This, in addition to a teaching job at Atlanta University, made for an extremely active year for DuBois in 1906." [5]

With all that on his plate, it's small wonder DuBois rapidly lost interest in his struggling little magazine. Soon, both he and Simon had effectively abandoned the venture, leaving Pace alone to battle for the *Moon's* survival. Dropping DuBois' idea of a truly national magazine, he switched its focus to the two core cities of Atlanta and Memphis, prioritizing features like his March 1906 profile of Robert Church's newly-formed Solvent Bank. The phenomenal workload he took on at this time is vividly described in this extract from George Washington Lee's 1934 book *Beale Street: Where the Blues Began*:

> *"With no money to pay the salaries of an editorial staff, most of the work of getting out the paper fell upon the shoulders of Harry Pace, who not only solicited and edited the material, but set its type, made up the paper, put it on the press, and ran it off. Pace worked twenty-four hours a day in trying to make this venture a success. Most of the time he was half-hungry and insufficiently clad. At four o'clock Saturday mornings the milkman would see him dragging a US mail sack down the streets to the post office."* [6]

Despite all Pace's efforts, the *Moon* was forced to close in August 1906, having published just 34 weekly issues and never selling more than 400 copies of any single one. Miriam DeCosta-Willis, who wrote a paper on the *Moon* for West Tennessee's Historical Society, concluded that the magazine's highbrow ambitions had been doomed from the start. "[Memphis] did not have the Black academic, cultural and economic infrastructure to sustain a national magazine aimed at the middle class", she writes. [7]

Rival Black publications, many of which had been glad to quote DuBois' *Moon* editorials just a few months earlier, were now quick to crow over its demise. "The 'Darker Races' are not responsive to the sort of 'record' Dr DuBois gave them," *New York Age* wrote in its leader column. Throwing in a snide reference to DuBois' "brave plea for Wall Street subsidy", it cheekily suggested he might like to hand over a list of the *Moon's* remaining subscribers so the *Age* could add them to its own readership. [8]

With the magazine now closed, a war of words broke out between Pace and Simon, each bombarding DuBois with their own letters and each determined to blame the other for everything that had gone wrong. "You sent Pace here to work outside," Simon complained. "During the whole time he never spent a whole week outside of the office. The whole thing was top-heavy. There was so much dignity and brain in the business that no-one could ask for a subscriber." A month later, he added that the terms DuBois had given Pace to get him on board "wrecked the business as surely as day follows night". [9]

Pace fired back in equally angry terms. "[Simon] lies unequivocally when he suggests that I did not contribute my full quota of labor," he assured DuBois. "I worked night and day until worn out from loss of sleep, overwork and lack of nourishment. I discontinued the *Moon* from sheer physical exhaustion while he lived well, smoked the best cigars every day and neglected the turning of the wheels." [10]

DuBois did his best to stay out of this row at first but finally came down on Pace's side – perhaps because Pace was the only one backing his points with hard figures from the *Moon's* accounts. As the year progressed, the three men's correspondence switched its focus from settling old scores to discussing whether the print shop itself could be saved and, if so, how its ownership should be split between them. But with Pace asking for a two-fifths share and Simon refusing to grant him more than a third, there was little hope of agreement there either. Finally, they gave up on any attempt to compromise and dissolved the partnership altogether. Simon moved to Atlanta, where – according to another letter from Pace to DuBois – he continued slinging mud at his former partners.

As all this ground on, Pace was left manning the dingy print offices in Beale Street, tying up loose ends in the *Moon's* admin, fending off its creditors and wondering what on earth he was going to do next. He'd given up a good teaching job and abandoned his dreams of law school to join DuBois' doomed little rag, and what did he have to show for it? His meagre savings were gone, his belly was empty, and his clothes barely fit for a scarecrow. Pace, then 22 years old, was by nature a very dapper young man, most comfortable when smartly – even formally – dressed, so this last privation must have hit him especially hard. Merah Stuart, who'd get to know him a few years later through their shared work in the insurance industry, later wrote of a night in November 1906 when Pace seriously considered taking his own life. "Dark failure stared him in the face, and he saw only one way out," Stuart writes. "There was the Mississippi River, swift and deep, right at the foot of Beale Street." [11]

Pace's dark thoughts that night were interrupted by a sudden burst of noise from Beale Street's partying crowds as two unexpected visitors entered the print shop: another pair of angry creditors, no doubt. Wearily, he got to his feet and prepared to face them. The first was a messenger boy with a telegram for him, who explained he could not hand it over till its 80 cents collection fee was paid. "Take it back," Pace told him. "I haven't a dime in the world. The only news that telegram could bring me would be bad news and I don't want any more of that."

That's when the second man spoke up. He was Ruben Ware, a cashier at Solvent Bank, who told the messenger to leave the telegram anyway. Paying the 80 cents from his own pocket, Ware took the message and held it out for Pace to open. When he still refused to accept it, Ware shrugged and tore it open himself. He scanned it quickly, laughed aloud and then read out its contents. It was a job offer from a Professor Allen at Lincoln Institute in Jefferson City, Missouri, who wanted Pace to join the faculty there. "Will you accept a position as professor of Latin and Greek at $110 per month?" Allen asked. "If so, report immediately."

The Lincoln Institute, created by Black soldiers after the Civil War to educate the children of freed slaves, was well on its way to winning university status by this time, and the salary was three times what Pace had been scraping by on at the *Moon*. This was a lifebelt to a drowning man. "But how can I take it?" he cried. "I have no clothes, no means of transportation, and no way to get any money."

Ware told him not to give up on the idea just yet and hurried off to see Thomas Hayes, the wealthy Black undertaker who Pace had persuaded to advertise in the *Moon* just a few months earlier. Hayes quickly agreed to pay for whatever new clothes Pace might need from a local tailor's shop. Ware lent him enough money to cover the rail fare to Jefferson City, throwing in a few dollars extra to tide him over there till his first pay cheque arrived. In the space of just a few days, Pace had gone from utter despair to the intoxicating promise of a whole new life – but Beale Street wasn't quite finished with him yet.

\*\*\*

Milton Clay, the owner of Beale Street's Panama Club, was also a director of Solvent Bank. Realising in 1907 that the bank needed to raise fresh capital, he remembered the determination Pace had shown while battling to save the *Moon* and persuaded Church they should offer him a job. Clay made the initial approach, dangling the prospect of rapid promotion to the board for Pace once he'd proved his worth. He also ensured Church followed this up with a letter of his own. Born a slave in 1839, Church was now one of the richest Black men in the South, so Clay knew just how much weight a personal letter from him would carry.

Even so, Pace was unconvinced. He was happy at Lincoln Institute, knew nothing about banking, and was already earning a good deal more than the $83 a month cashier's salary Solvent wanted him to start on. "I have not yet accepted the position, he told DuBois in August 1907. "I do not think I shall, because of my inexperience, but it is pleasing to know that I have the opportunity." Reminding DuBois of his recent press statement about the *Moon's* collapse – a statement which Pace felt unfairly handed him the blame – he also took this chance to rub his old mentor's nose in it a little. "After working as hard as I did and sacrificing everything to keep the *Moon* alive, it cut me very severely to be held up to the world as one devoid of ability and judgement," he wrote. "I feel this letter, coming entirely unsolicited from the strongest business interest in Memphis, is a vindication." [12]

It was Pace's characteristic mixture of idealism and ambition that made him change his mind about the Solvent offer. The excitement of living by his wits in keeping the *Moon* alive had awoken an entrepreneurial instinct in the young man, revealing strengths he'd never known he had and offering thrills a quiet career in teaching could not match. He could see that Solvent was exactly the kind of bank Black savers and businesses needed if they were ever going to improve their prospects in America. Where else was he going to be promised a fast track to the boardroom in a company like that?

In the end, he accepted the Solvent job and returned to Beale Street after only a year in Jefferson City. By November 1907, he'd been elected as a Solvent director and was again writing to DuBois about his prospects there. "Church is still in charge but as soon as the papers are completed in my bond arrangements and I have become thoroughly acquainted with the business, I will take charge," he said. In the four years that followed, he engineered an increase in Solvent's assets from $50,000 to $600,000, making it one of the four largest Black-owned banks in America. The liquidity problems it had recruited Pace to solve were now a thing of the past. [13]

DuBois had launched a new magazine called *Crisis* by this time, a better-funded and ultimately much more successful version of the *Moon*, which profiled Pace in its October 1911 issue. "Mr Harry H. Pace is one of the most successful young Negro businessmen in the country," it declared. But if DuBois hoped this profile would flatter Pace into renewing their old partnership, he'd soon be disappointed. When he contacted Pace asking him to swap his 1911 Solvent salary of $200 a month for half that sum running *Crisis* instead, Pace had no difficulty whatsoever in turning him down.

# Father of the blues

*"A rain of silver dollars began to fall
around the outlandish, stomping feet. The
dancers went wild. Dollars, quarters, halves –
the shower grew heavier and continued so long
I strained my neck to get a better look. There
before the boys lay more money than my nine
musicians were being paid for the entire
engagement. [...] Their music wanted
polishing, but it contained the essence. Folks
would pay money for it."*

**- WC Handy on first encountering a
Mississippi string band (from *Father of the
Blues*).**

WC Handy was a born musician. Entering the world as
William Christopher Handy on November 16, 1873, in
Florence, Alabama, he was the son of a strict father named
Charles and his wife Elizabeth. Charles did his best to
discourage the boy's early interest in music, forcing him to
swap a childhood guitar William had bought with his own
money for an improving dictionary instead. But it was
Elizabeth's heritage which won out. Her own father had
played the fiddle at barn dances, and it was his spirit she
could see animating her young son too.

Handy was still a teenager when he launched on his

first musical adventure, running away to perform with a touring minstrel show. That ended badly when he found himself stranded in a strange town and was forced to return home with his tail between his legs. He followed that up with a spell as a teacher, then worked in an iron foundry for while before taking to the road once more with a vocal quartet in the Spring of 1893. He'd remain in more or less constant motion round the US with one band or another for the next 20 years, climbing from his initial role as just one more singing guitarist to become a bandleader with a full dance orchestra of his own.

Whichever city he visited, Handy would cock an ear to the local street music he heard played by buskers and saloon singers there. Most people were quick to dismiss this music as trash, but Handy saw real value in it and was ready to take its lessons on board. One key moment came in his early days as a penniless touring musician, when he found himself standing outside a brightly-lit St Louis bar, broke, hungry and without a shirt beneath his tattered coat.

"While occupied with my own miseries during that sojourn, I had seen a woman whose pain seemed even greater," he writes. "She had tried to take the edge off her grief by heavy drinking, but it hadn't worked. Stumbling along the poorly lighted street, she muttered as she walked, 'Ma man's got a heart like a rock cast in de sea'." Twenty years later, that line would inspire Handy's own composition *St Louis Blues* and take him another step towards finding his own musical language. Looking back on the St Louis encounter in 1941, he acknowledged its importance. "My song was taking shape," he writes. "I had now settled upon the mood." [1]

A second epiphany came in Tutwiler, Mississippi. Dozing at the railway station as he waited for his train, Handy was awoken by an unfamiliar sound. "A lean, loose-jointed Negro had commenced plunking a guitar beside me while I slept," he recalls. "His clothes were rags; his feet peeped out of his shoes. His face had on it some of the sadness of the ages. As he played, he pressed a knife on the strings of a guitar in a manner popularized by Hawaiian guitarists who used steel bars. The effect was unforgettable. His song, too, struck me instantly. 'Goin' where the Southern cross the Dog'. The singer repeated the line three times, accompanying himself on the guitar with the weirdest music I ever heard." Once again, Handy filed away this revelation for future use. [2, 3]

Soon after this incident, Handy's orchestra played a date in Cleveland, Mississippi, where they found themselves blown off stage by a local string band trio. "They had the stuff the people wanted," Handy writes. "The old conventional music was well and good and had its place, no denying that, but there was no virtue in being blind when you had good eyes." Now thoroughly convinced that blues music had a commercial potential no-one else had spotted, he was soon arranging traditional songs like *Make Me Down a Pallet on Your Floor* for his ensembles and selling the resulting tunes as fully-notated sheet music to the music publishers of the day. [4]

Handy certainly didn't invent the blues – no one person can claim that - but he was the first man to bring these informal street songs into the commercial music industry. In 1905 he moved to Memphis, basing himself on Beale Street where he gathered a menagerie of players who could be grouped together into anything from a modest quartet to a full 20-piece dance orchestra. By 1907 he was one of the best-known and best-loved musicians in the whole city.

\*\*\*

One day in 1907, Pace was working in the banking hall at Solvent when a chubby, balding Black man with a moustache approached him to discuss the possibility of a mortgage loan – and he realised he was talking to WC Handy. Pace was not yet 25 and Handy already in his mid-thirties, but the two men hit it off immediately.

Pace had dabbled in writing song lyrics for years, and occasionally sang a number or two at small social gatherings. "[He was] a handsome man of striking personality and definite musical leanings," Handy recalls in his autobiography. "He had written some first-date song lyrics and was in demand as a vocal soloist at church programs and Sunday night concerts. It was natural, if not inevitable, that he and I should gravitate together. We spoke the same language."

Pace's own preference was for the sentimental parlour songs of the late 19th century rather than the boisterous street music Handy was already starting to document, but the older man could see his talent nonetheless. The pair started to collaborate just a few months after they first met. Their first song together was 1907's *In The Cotton Fields of Dixie*, an unremarkable plantation song, which they placed with George Jaberg's publishing firm in Cincinnati. Handy later came to regret this deal, calling Jaberg a "song-shark" who'd "fleeced" them by failing to distribute or promote the song as he'd promised to do – an early lesson for both men in the thieving ways of the music business. [5, 6]

*Cotton Fields* has not survived, but we can get a sense of Pace's lyrics from another of his collaborations with Handy: a 1917 song they called *Thinking of Thee*.

*When the stars bestud the skies far, far away,*
*Loving thoughts of thee arise, bright as the day,*
*Lyra in the distance blinking,*

*Tries to lure me with her winking,*
*But of thee alone I'm thinking,*
*Tenderly.*

Lyra is a constellation named for the ancient Greek myth of Orpheus & Euridice, so we can see the evidence of Pace's classical education here. What's most striking, though, is how mimsy and toothless his lyrics seem compared to the gritty rough-and-tumble of Handy's own *Beale Street Blues* from the same year:

*You'll see pretty browns in beautiful gowns,*
*You'll see tailor-mades and hand-me-downs,*
*You'll meet honest men and pickpockets skilled,*
*You'll find business never ceases till somebody gets*
*killed!*

Despite this sharp difference in their style and preoccupations, Handy found genuine value in Pace's writing. "I liked very much the style of his early lyrics," he writes in *Father of the Blues*. "They were a departure from the levee songs I knew, and I was delighted to make musical settings for them." If anything, he adds, Pace's compositions might have fared better if Handy's name hadn't been so firmly linked to blues in the public's mind. This set up an expectation for their collaborative songs which Pace's lyrics could not help but disappoint, Handy suggests. [7]

The first of Handy's own tunes to spread his name beyond Memphis was an instrumental called *Mr Crump*, which he wrote as a campaign tune for the city's 1909 mayoral candidate Edward Crump. It was common then for political candidates to buy a theme song like this for themselves which would be played at rallies to stir up the crowd before the speeches began. In this case, the tune proved popular enough for Handy to start playing it at his own gigs too. Once, he confesses, he even slipped it into the programme at an event held for one of Crump's opponents.

Crump positioned himself as the reform candidate, promising he'd introduce strict ordinances to crack down on the noisy chaos of Beale Street. That went down well enough with voters who were anxious about the city's respectability, but it was never going to be a popular policy with Handy's fans. "I heard various comments from the crowds around us, and even from my own men, which seemed to express their own feelings about reform," he writes. "Most of these comments had been sung, impromptu, to my music." Handy pulled together the best of these remarks, adjusted their scansion where necessary and came up verses like these:

*Mr Crump don't 'low no easy riders here,*
*We don't care what Mr Crump don't 'low,*
*We gonna barrel house anyhow,*
*Mr Crump don't 'low no easy riders here,*

*Crump don't 'low it, ain't gonna have it,*
*We don't care what Mr Crump don't 'low,*
*We gonna barrel house anyhow,*
*Mr Crump can go catch himself some air.*

"Luckily for us, Mr Crump himself didn't hear us singing these words," Handy writes. "But we were hired to help put over his campaign, and since I knew that reform was about as palatable to Beale Street voters as castor oil, I was sure those reassuring words would do him more good than harm." He was right: Crump not only won the mayoral election in 1909 but remained a power in the city right through to his death in 1954. Handy later revived his campaign tune under the name we know it by today: *Memphis Blues*. Once again, though, he found himself cheated by a white music publisher.

"He self-published it but sold the copyright for a very inadequate sum to a canny white publisher who, while visiting Memphis, assured Handy it was too difficult to play and wouldn't sell," writes Handy expert Elliott Hurwitt. "Handy would never fall for such a ruse again." In this case, there was some consolation, though it came in the form of fame rather than hard cash. The publisher hired *Melancholy Baby's* George Norton to put words to Handy's tune, and it was Norton who had the idea of promoting Handy as the bandleader everyone visiting Memphis just had to hear. "This made Handy instantly famous nationwide," Hurwitt adds. "It also made the song a talisman of the city." [8]

Pace had his own encounter with Crump in the following mayoral election. He'd created a new organization called Colored Citizens of Memphis, with himself as president, and used that position to quiz both Crump and his opponent about what they'd do for the city's Black people. "The other candidate promises everything and I fear he will do nothing," Pace reported back. "This red-headed fellow [Crump] frankly declines to promise some of the things we want but convinces me he will fulfil the promises he did make." With his reputation at Solvent Bank still growing, and now with a finger in the city's politics too, Pace was extending his network of useful contacts every day.

When Robert Church, Solvent's founder, died in 1912, Pace found himself thoroughly unimpressed by the bank's new senior management and let it be known he was ready to consider any new opportunities that might be out there. It wasn't long before he was offered the job of company secretary at the Black-owned Standard Life in Atlanta. It meant another pay cut – this one from Solvent's $2,400 a year to just $2,000 – and moving to a new city, but he decided to take it anyway.

It turned out to be another rescue mission. "In Atlanta, he found that Standard Life had on hand only $1,700 after the required deposit had been made with the state," Merah Stuart writes. "It was necessary to find $50,000 from some other source before the company could meet the tests of a state examination." Pace conceived and executed a plan to sort out this funding crisis and then set about installing the business systems and departmental structure needed to put Standard on a proper professional footing. "Around his constructive ability, more than around any other man, has Standard Life been built," the *Atlanta Independent* wrote a few years later.

One of the major obstacles Pace had to overcome in order to save Standard Life was the company's own founder and now president Heman Perry. "Perry was impatient of details and the regulations of accounting," Stuart writes. "He was inclined to invade any fund or department and make use of any available means to realize his dreams. The irregularities and complications resultant from such procedure met with strong resistance from his business-minded secretary."

That conflict would come to the boil soon enough: first Pace had a new venture in mind he wanted to discuss with Handy back in Memphis.

*The young Harry Pace. Art by Karl Stevens.*

# Pace & Handy Inc.

*"These were the glory days of Tin Pan Alley when music publishers such as Leo Feist, Harry von Tilzer and a young Irving Berlin ruled the industry with an iron fist. Pace & Handy fit in with those established houses because it already owned established hits and specialized in black songwriters, which the larger publishing houses rarely handled."*

**- Mark Berresford & Russ Shor in *Black Swan: The Record Label of the Harlem Renaissance* (1996).**

Both Handy and Pace knew from their own experience how hard it was for Black songwriters to get a fair shake from the white-owned music publishers of the early 1900s. Then the only game in town, these firms rarely condescended to publish a Black musician's work at all and, even when they did, routinely cheated him of the song's revenue at every turn. Why did they do this? One very simple reason: they knew the law would let them to get away with it.

Pace's solution to this injustice was to suggest he and Handy set up a publishing company of their own – and one which specialized in working with the Black songwriters and bandleaders the white firms preferred to ignore. As America's first Black-owned music publisher, they'd be able to ensure that these neglected talents were treated fairly for once and that the money generated by their songs remained in the Black community. Handy's growing stock of his own popular tunes was there to give the new firm's catalogue a sound foundation, and his contacts among Black musicians all over the US was sure to pull in plenty of clients. Pace's contribution would be to raise the start-up funds needed, set up all the admin and act as the company's business manager. Meanwhile, he'd continue at Standard Life in Atlanta and Handy would continue touring with his band. Handy liked the idea and, in 1912, the fledgling firm of Pace & Handy began trading.

Handy's band then had a Memphis residency at the Alaskan Roof Garden nightclub atop the Falls Building on North Front Street. This was a whites-only club - at least as far as the audience was concerned - and Handy's rising star there meant very few Black people in the city now got a chance to hear his orchestra play. Black promotors either assumed the white audience had priced Handy's band beyond their own reach, or simply wrote them off as an act only white people enjoyed.

*Memphis Blues* changed all that. Every musician in the city began playing their own version of the song, often in a rather garbled form, and this created a big appetite among Black audiences determined to hear the composer's own orchestra tackling it as it was meant to be heard. Suddenly, Black promoters were keen to book Handy's band too, and started putting up the kind of cash that made them impossible to ignore. "They made every effort to secure our services, offering as much as twice the fee we received from the white folks," Handy writes.

Finally, he agreed to a gig at a Black theatre in Atlanta, which was scheduled for May 12, 1916 and heavily promoted there. When white bookers in the city heard about this, they contacted Pace and suggested he persuade his partner to cancel this concert and take up their offer of using Atlanta's 7,000-seat white auditorium instead. This was the venue where New York's Metropolitan Opera appeared whenever it visited the city, making it a pretty daunting prospect for a glorified dance band. Handy was skeptical, if not downright terrified, but Pace managed to talk him round and the venue was duly switched. When Atlanta's liberal newspaper, *The Constitution*, attacked this decision, Pace simply ensured the event's advertising spend went to two of the city's rival papers instead. This was business, after all.

The concert, when it came, was a triumph. "The storm broke when we played *Memphis Blues* and had to repeat it nine times," Handy writes. "After that, it was goodbye to the printed program. We played only requests, and these called for blues, blues and more blues. People seemed to be starving for blues. My daughter Katherine, then only twelve, sang *St Louis Blues* and, for encores, *Joe Turner* and again *Memphis Blues*. They wouldn't let us stop." The gig produced rave reviews in all three of Atlanta's city papers, each of which splashed the coverage on the front page. Even the *Constitution* was forced to drop its earlier objections. "At last, we see the democracy of ragtime," its headline declared.

Pace staged a little show of his own during the Atlanta visit, his aim being to ensure that everyone there saw his partner as a massive and untouchable star. He'd recruited a few friends to join him in posing as Handy's bodyguards, clustering tightly around him every time he stepped out of his dressing room to form a security cordon against the rabid fans they seemed to fear might pounce at any moment. Whenever Handy needed to move from his hotel to the venue and back, they hustled him into a private car with great urgency and peered anxiously up and down the street before escorting him out again. None of this was remotely necessary, but it did make Handy look like a celebrity, and that was what Pace wanted. "I detected a box office twinkle in my partner's eye," Handy writes. "We were kept over and played Atlanta for a week."

The band was due to move on to North Carolina next, where it had a gig booked on the state's university campus in Chapel Hill. But Handy found his musicians rebelling. They had so much money in their pockets from the Atlanta engagement and had garnered so much praise for their performance there that all they wanted to do now was get back to Beale Street and show off their new status. When Handy discussed this problem with Pace, he suggested cancelling the Chapel Hill performance outright and letting the guys return to Memphis as soon as they liked. P&H was doing well enough to support Handy full-time now, he argued, and its prospects for further growth all lay in New York where most of the music business was based. It was time for Handy to give up his exhausting life as a touring bandleader, move to Manhattan and set up a permanent P&H office there. Pace would quit Standard Life and join him in New York as soon as the publishing company was big enough to support him too.

The idea of cancelling a gig – any gig – was anathema to Handy, but he could see the appeal of this idea all the same. He was in his early forties now, thoroughly sick of the constant hassle of herding recalcitrant musicians together on the road, and liked the thought of sleeping in his own bed rather than relying on a string of cheap hotels. He agreed to Pace's plan and opened the company's New York office in 1918. [1]

These were P&H's golden days. Handy was turning out hit after hit, with 1912's *Memphis Blues* and 1914's *St Louis Blues* quickly joined by *Joe Turner's Blues (1915), Yellow Dog Blues* (1915), *Beale Street Blues* (1917) and *Harlem Blues* (1918). Other writers in the P&H stable were doing well too. Eddie Green's 1917 song *A Good Man is Hard to Find*, which Handy had bought for the firm just before the office move, was quickly adopted by Sophie Tucker, then a huge vaudeville star. She'd liked the song so much when she heard Alberta Hunter introduce it in Chicago that she learned it by rote and had it in her act even before the P&H sheet music was out. Handy splashed her picture on all his ads for the song and added it to the sheet music's title page too, racking up sales of 500,000 copies in its first year. Now a little strap line was appearing beneath the P&H logo on all its publications: "Home of the Blues".

It's hard for us to understand now just how lucrative sheet music sales could be for a successful songwriter in the 1910s and 1920s. Hurwitt estimates that *St Louis Blues* alone gave Handy an income of $50,000 a year, and as record sales began to enter the picture the money flowed in even faster. Earl Fuller's 1917 disc of *Beale Street Blues* and the Joseph Smith Orchestra's 1919 recording of *Yellow Dog Blues* both left Handy rubbing his eyes in disbelief when their first royalty cheques came in. The Fuller disc's first cheque gave Handy $1,857 when he'd been expecting something more like $200, and Smith's disc immediately brought in $7,000. Multiply that figure by 15 and you'll get an idea of its spending power today.

It was the size of the *Yellow Dog Blues* cheque which stunned Handy most of all, convincing him at first that it must have come to the wrong address. "Then I saw it was for Pace & Handy Music Co," he writes. "Finally, I saw the number of *Yellow Dog* records that had been sold – unbelievable. These records created a demand for orchestrations and sheet music in the thousands. Before our printers could deliver ten thousand copies, we had orders for one hundred thousand. Money was pouring in."

It was around this time that Pace arranged one of

the Handy Band's own first recording sessions. While in New York on Standard Life business, he sold Columbia on paying the band to travel up from Memphis and spend a few days recording at the label's Manhattan studio. In putting this deal together, Pace again proved his value as a negotiator. "The fee seemed to me a fabulous sum to pay twelve men travelling to and from New York City for three days' work," Handy writes. Columbia got its money's worth too: the sessions produced 15 tracks in all, eight of which had the all-important word "blues" in their title. [2]

It wasn't long before the company's songs got it noticed overseas too. Opening the post one morning, they discovered a letter from Buckingham Palace. It was from one of King George V's musicians there, who complained that what he called "the nigger bands" in London often got hold of P&H's best tunes before he did. Surely they could make arrangements to give his own orchestra a copy of every new piece so the British Royal Family could hear them first? Pace wrote back, explaining that, seeing as how both he and Handy were Black themselves, the King's musicians would just have to wait their turn like everyone else. [3]

While all this was happening in Memphis and New York, Pace was equally busy in Atlanta. He got involved in a successful campaign to prevent the city's school board diverting funds away from Black pupils, and then joined with other Standard Life employees to form Atlanta's first NAACP branch. Pace was the branch's president and one of his Standard Life hires was branch secretary. That young man – whose name was Walter White – joined the NAACP's national office a couple of years later and went on to serve as the organisation's leader for over 25 years. [4]

It was also in Atlanta that Pace met Ethlynde Bibb, a fair-skinned young Black woman who was every bit his equal in education, refinement and determination.

Ethlynde's grandfather was Joseph Bibb, a Harvard-educated lawyer who'd go on to found a radical Black newspaper called *The Chicago Whip,* her father Joseph was a prominent preacher and her mother Viola a society figure in her own right. Harry and Ethlynde married in June 1917 when he was 33 and she was 24. They honeymooned in Florida, but Pace was forced to cut the trip short when word reached him that his enemies at Standard Life were plotting a coup.

There were two rival factions at work in the company by then, one supporting Perry's freewheeling ways and the other backing Pace's drive for greater discipline and professionalism. When Pace returned to Atlanta from his truncated honeymoon, he found things had sunk to such a point that Perry was barely speaking to him. He stuck out the situation at Standard Life until 1920, then packed up and left for New York with Ethlynde and their two-year old son Harry Jr. Just as he'd promised Handy a few years earlier, he was now ready to make P&H his main concern.

Handy had already found a house for the family a few doors from his own in a swanky stretch of Harlem's West 138th street which everyone called Strivers' Row. "Things were busy and the business needed him," Handy writes. "He came and took over the house, giving up his work with the Standard Life." With Pace now able to devote all his efforts to the company, the future looked brighter than ever. Soon, they were confident enough to give up their original New York office above Times Square's Gaiety Theatre to take over a whole building on the same block.

# Too much money

*"By the end of World War 1, the US music industries produced goods worth more than $335m; never before had those industries exercised such cultural authority or financial influence in American life. [...] The music industries were not an equal opportunity employer, however. [...] When African-Americans did make records, the recordings were limited to comedy or novelty styles."*

**- David Suisman, *Co-workers in the Kingdom of Culture* (2004).**

For the first decade of the twentieth century, what few phonograph records were available offered mostly operatic material and light classics. Record players were expensive novelties and the discs themselves seen mainly as a promotional gimmick to encourage equipment sales. A few nostalgic songs of the old country, aimed at European immigrants to the US, started to appear on record in the 1910s but Black artists were still allowed to record only the demeaning "coon songs" and comic numbers people knew from the minstrel shows. Record companies – all white-owned of course – were terrified that adding Black singers to their roster in any other capacity would lead to Southern distributors dropping those titles, or even refusing to deal with the label altogether.

That began to change with the outbreak of the First World War in 1914, when the threat from German U-boats in the Atlantic choked off European immigration to the US. Factories in New York, Chicago and Detroit were forced to recruit Black Southerners to man their assembly lines instead, creating a second wave of what we now call "the great migration" of rural Black people to the Northern cities. They'd still face white bigotry when they got there, of course, but at least it was a little less pronounced in the North, and that opened new opportunities to enjoy life, as well as a chance to improve your own and your family's prospects. Half a million African-Americans travelled north between 1914 and 1916, with a million more joining them in the decade that followed. Often for the first time in their lives, former plantation workers and sharecroppers found themselves with a little spare cash to spend on whatever they liked.

This was a big enough change to create a thriving new market for all sorts of modest consumer goods in the cities where they settled. Meanwhile, the record industry was still busy pushing Black performers to the margin, taking hot compositions from the early Black jazz bands but almost always using white bands to record them. The flood of comic minstrel songs continued, but even these were often recorded by white vaudeville performers who adopted crude "darky" accents as soon as they stepped into the recording studio and portrayed their Black characters as either clowns or children. When Black people understandably declined to buy these discs, the record labels simply took this as confirmation that they'd been right all along. Black people clearly didn't buy records, so why bother trying to cater for them?

Many of the people running the record companies hated the thought of a Black-owned publisher earning royalties from their discs' sales, and some took this resentment so far they banned their artists from recording any P&H song. Even when the company did succeed in getting one of its songs recorded, its distribution was sometimes sabotaged for the same reason. "It was my job as President of the Company to contact all phonograph companies so that our own numbers might be recorded from time to time," Pace recalls in a 1939 letter to the author Roi Ottley. "I ran up against a color line that was very severe." [1]

Sometimes the harassment became alarmingly personal. One evening, Handy and Pace looked out of their office window to see a group of white men pointing up at the building from the other side of the street. Handy recognised their leader as a senior manager at Victor Records, who seemed to be very angry about something.

Marion Harris, a popular white singer whose performance of jazz and blues songs was authentic enough to convince many listeners she must be Black, had just left Victor to record for Columbia instead. According to Handy, she'd quit because Victor so resented paying P&H royalties that it refused to let her record *St Louis Blues*. At Columbia there were no such restrictions, so she ditched Victor and recorded the song there instead.

Pace and Handy watched as the executive below crossed to a nearby payphone, and a moment later their office phone rang. Pace picked it up and the Victor man instantly started berating him about Harris and her move. "The conversation became definitely unpleasant," Handy writes. Leaving the building for his journey home that night, Handy found the same man still waiting outside, who confronted him in the street and began ranting again. "He said we had made ten times too much money from his phonograph company," Handy writes. "Nothing more came of the incident at that time, but already the air was charged."

It was a frustrating time. Handy's musical connections ensured he ran into most of the best Black songwriters and performers, and he could see how popular their work was with live audiences. P&H would send demonstration pianists round the stores selling sheet music in all America's big cities to show just how good the tunes on offer sounded. Whenever it was a blues song being played, Handy noticed, Black crowds would gather outside the shop purely for the pleasure of hearing it. He knew they'd buy records too, if given half a chance, but white-owned label executives erected a brick wall very time he and Pace tried to move in that direction. P&H had a host of great new songs in its publishing catalogue and knew exactly the Black artists needed to do those songs justice, and yet they were blocked at every turn.

Things started to look a lot brighter in 1919, when a string of legal challenges led to Victor and Columbia losing their exclusive patents on the manufacture of both records themselves and the machines needed to play them. This opened the way for a crowd of small, feisty rivals like Okeh and Gennett to enter the market. These new arrivals were full of fresh ideas, such as Okeh owner Otto Heinemann's early plans for a mobile recording unit to gather music from all across the US. Often, they had to improvise, as Gennett discovered when boxcars on the railway line near its Indiana recording studio turned out to be audible on the finished discs. The fidelity of the recordings these new labels produced couldn't always match what the big boys were achieving, but the important thing was that Victor and Columbia's stranglehold on the industry had been broken at last.

Gennett, Okeh and the rest knew they would have to be imaginative, aggressive and adventurous if they hoped to survive. Above all, with every established star already signed up by the majors and no funds to buy these big names away, the new labels were forced to find talent of their own. Heinemann, for example, was quick to sign unknown artists singing in German, Czech or Polish, knowing there was a neglected market for these discs among America's most recent immigrants. The time was ripe for a breakthrough in P&H's style of music too, but it was one of their Black rivals who'd snatch the prize. [2, 3]

# The first blues record

*"You could walk down the streets of any Black neighbourhood in the United States and you would hear* [Crazy Blues] *being played. You would hear it pouring out of the windows of every building. At a time when Black people were not in motion pictures, when they really weren't being represented in any of the major forms of entertainment, suddenly here were their voices."*

**- Blues historian Marybeth Hamilton speaking to the author in March 2007.**

Perry Bradford started as a pianist in the minstrel shows and began writing his own blues songs when he arrived in New York in 1910. By the time the new labels started up, he was convinced there was a market for records in the Black community but knew these new buyers would not surface until the industry supplied something they wanted to hear.

This was the era not just of dance bands like Handy's playing the blues, but also of the smaller nightclub ensembles performing cabaret blues – a genre where Black female singers were always the biggest stars. "Blues" in this context meant not the music we associate with Robert Johnson, Muddy Waters and John Lee Hooker today – none of whom would start playing till the 1930s – but something much more like an early form of jazz. The women fronting cabaret blues bands would mix sophisticated ballads with darker sexual songs, offering their predominantly white male audiences an intoxicating thrill. That excitement was only heightened by the fact that so many of the clubs they performed in were owned by gangsters. Alberta Hunter was just one of the singers at these clubs who found her set interrupted by gunshots in the audience one night, and a man slumped dead at her feet when the lights came back on. [1, 2]

A life like that left the singers few illusions, and they knew just when to insert a gut-bucket roar into their delivery, giving the boiling jazz behind them a horny, primitive charge no other singers would have been allowed to get away with. Any white woman singing like that would have been condemned as a hopeless slut, while a Black man expressing such frank sexual power was thought far too threatening for white audiences to accept. And at this point, it was very much the white audience which mattered.

Upmarket cabaret venues like the soon-to-be-launched Cotton Club were racially segregated, using Black musicians and singers on stage, but allowing only whites in the audience. Even where no official segregation was imposed, the prices were kept too high for all but a tiny handful of Black people to afford. Outside the big cities, there were only the touring tent shows. Once in a while, these shows would slip a cabaret blues act in among its minstrel sketches and marching bands, but that was a low-rent circuit any established name preferred to avoid.

All this meant that, for the vast majority of African-Americans, the biggest cabaret blues stars were just names in a newspaper, who they could never hope to hear singing for themselves. Simply seeing those Black women succeed in a white man's world offered some kind of satisfaction, but how much more thrilling it would be to hear them perform! Give these neglected listeners a genuine taste of their own music on record, Bradford argued, sung and played with all the raw glory of its live shows, and they'd strip the shelves bare.

Like Pace & Handy, Bradford had a stash of songs which would be ideal for this new market, plus plenty of contacts among the Black singers and musicians who could do his songs full justice. He was ideally placed to pair the right combination of musicians with exactly the song that combo needed to shine, creating a deal Bradford could then present at the studio door as a single neat package. Any rational label would have bitten his hand off at this opportunity, but when it came to Black performers, rationality was not the industry's first concern. They'd already shown just how determined they were not to give Black talent an airing.

Bradford knew that, if he was ever going to succeed in breaking that embargo, he'd have to sell the idea on strictly commercial grounds, stressing the vast new market he was offering these labels a chance to reach. He was also smart enough to get the two most popular Black vaudeville performers of the day on board, persuading both the singer/comedian Bert Williams and the song and dance man Bill Robinson to let him use their names while pitching his project around. Williams and Robinson were no fools and must have realised Bradford would drop heavy hints at every meeting about them signing up with whichever label was brave enough to take a lead in releasing genuine Black music. Bradford wanted to focus attention on the point that there was money to be made here and having some big earners like these two in his corner stressed that all the more. [3]

Even so, there was no denying that any label taking Bradford's idea on was running a risk. Just one all-Black disc on the label could lead to their whole distribution network in the South walking away and perhaps to a label-wide boycott from white record buyers too. Victor and Columbia had too much invested in the industry's existing infrastructure to risk any upset, but Bradford hoped one of their fledgling rivals would be more receptive. In his 1965 book *Born with the Blues*, he describes how he "walked out two pairs of shoes" trailing round from one label to the next, saying he was often turned away with derisive laughter or a casual insult. And then, in 1920, someone at Okeh decided to give him a chance.

That someone was Fred Hager, the label's white studio director. Bradford's first suggestion of an all-Black ensemble – singer included - was still a bit too rich for the company's blood, but Hager did agree to let him record a Black cabaret singer called Mamie Smith cutting two of Bradford's songs with the label's all-white Rega Orchestra backing her. Even that was quite a brave move, as Bradford acknowledges in his book. "[Hager was] worried because of the many threatening letters he had received from some Northern and Southern pressure groups warning him not to have any truck with colored girls in the recording field," he writes. "Okeh products – phonograph machines and records – would be boycotted. It took a man with plenty of nerves and guts to buck these powerful groups and make the historical decision which would echo round the world. He pried open that old prejudiced door for the first colored girl, Mamie Smith."

The resulting disc, which paired Bradford's *That Thing Called Love* with *You Can't Keep a Good Man Down*, was released in early 1920. It now sounds like a conventional jazz record of the day, with a slight bluesy feel to it but breaking no new musical ground. It did have a Black singer at its helm, though – the record's credited to Mamie Smith as a solo artist – and allowed her to perform with none of the demeaning comic tricks white listeners were used to. It sold well enough to give Bradford a bit of extra pull at the label, but Okeh ascribed its succuss to his songwriting rather than Smith's performance and suggested he use Sophie Tucker for the planned follow-up: another Bradford number called *Harlem Blues*.

Tucker was a former blackface singer who'd continued to sing blues and ragtime after abandoning the make-up. She was a big name, but a million miles away from the authentic Black voice Bradford wanted to capture, so he must have been secretly delighted when she turned out to be unavailable. Hager agreed to him bringing in Mamie Smith again as a replacement but insisted he change the song's name to the more innocuous *Crazy Blues*.

Smith returned to Okeh's New York studio in August 1920, and this time Bradford was left alone to build a real Black jazz band behind her, led by stride piano legend Willie "The Lion" Smith. He marked the band's greater importance in this session by crediting the record to "Mamie Smith & her Jazz Hounds" and encouraged them to cut loose in the studio in a way that had never been permitted before. The result was a vast improvement on Smith's earlier outing, with her voice taking on a rougher, more abrasive edge, and the band lurching round every corner on two skidding wheels. Smith's experience making herself heard in noisy clubs gives her voice a throaty blare which survives even on what now sounds like a very lo-fi recording. This, combined with the touch of pained, angry vibrato she adds to key words ensures she gets full value from Bradford's gritty lyrics, threatening first suicide and then murder: [4]

*I went to the railroad,*
*Hang my head on the track,*
*Thought about my daddy,*

*I gladly snatched it back,*
*Now my babe's gone,*
*And gave me the sack,*


*I'm gonna do like a Chinaman,*
*Go and get some hop,*
*Get myself a gun and shoot myself a cop,*
*I ain't had nothin' but bad news,*
*Now I've got the crazy blues.* [5]


Dope Andrews' trombone honks like a goose behind her as she sings, and clarinetist Ernest Elliot fills the top register with a swarm of urgent notes. It's as if everyone present has kicked off a pair of tight shoes and decided that now, at last, is the time to have some fun. *Crazy Blues* is still recognised today as the first real blues record and its November 1920 release was an essential precursor to everything that's followed. Recorded blues was now firmly on the road that would lead to Robert Johnson's legendary Hellhound sessions of 1936, and popular music would never be the same again.

Okeh couldn't afford to spend much money promoting its records but articles in the Black press made sure everyone knew what a game-changing release this was. Late in 1920, Manhattan's *New Amsterdam News* reported it had sold 50,000 copies in Harlem alone, lending some credence to Bradford's own claim that it shifted 75,000 copies in its first month. Sales of 100,000 were enough for a big hit in those days, and by Christmas Day, *Crazy Blues'* total is said to have passed that milestone too. Sales figures from this era are notoriously unreliable, but the best indications are that it racked up 120,000 sales by the end of January 1921 and perhaps twice that number before it was done. Bradford netted about $53,000 in royalties from the disc, and angrily rejected Okeh's attempts to make him sign any part of that income away. [6]

Some bought the record even when they had nothing to play it on, content to bring it to a more fortunate neighbour's party or simply to let everyone see them carrying it around in the street. "It became a kind of talisman," the blues historian Marybeth Hamilton told me. "To have this object, even if you couldn't get the sound out of it, was a kind of validation that you mattered." [7]

"There's fourteen million Negroes in our great country," Bradford pointed out to one journalist. "And they will buy records if recorded by one of their own. We are the only folks who can sing and interpret hot jazz songs just off the griddle." Suddenly, every record company in America was scrabbling to target this new market. A flood of cheap phonographs was rushed into production and salesmen began hawking the machines round the Black neighbourhoods they'd previously spurned. Meanwhile, scouts from every label – Columbia and Victor included – were scouring the country's vaudeville halls, nightclub dives and tent shows for the undiscovered Black talent everyone was now desperate to put on disc.

Pace watched all this unfold from P&H's offices and, as 1920 drew to an end, he decided he was ready to make his move.

*Fletcher Henderson. Art by Karl Stevens.*

# Piano man

> *"Professor Henderson as principal hired the*
> *best music teachers for his school and saw to it*
> *that his children took lessons from them at*
> *home as well. Fletcher started lessons at the*
> *age of six and, like most boys that age, wanted*
> *to quit, but his father made him continue until*
> *he was thirteen. [...] Even after his sons*
> *became famous, he would not allow them to*
> *play jazz in his house."*
>
> **- Walter Allen in his 1973 book *Hendersonia*.**

Fletcher Henderson was born on December 18, 1897 in
Cuthbert, Georgia, which makes him just 23 years old
when Pace decided to poach him from P&H for a job at the
new record label he was now planning. Like Pace himself,
Henderson was fair-skinned, a graduate of Atlanta
University and fonder of classical music than the rough and
tumble of the blues. The two men's Georgia hometowns
were less than 200 miles apart and both had lived in Atlanta
between 1916 and 1920, when Henderson was a student
there and Pace at Standard Life. Even with the 13-year gap
in their ages, Pace must have felt very much at home with
this polite, studious young man.

Henderson had joined P&H in the Fall of 1920 as
one of the company's three in-house pianists, hired to

transform the dry dots on paper into a tune both the music shop owners who hosted him and their customers might want to buy. His musical talent was obvious, but he'd come to New York with a very different career in mind.

His father, Fletcher Snr, ran Cuthbert's Howard Normal School, a prestigious private academy for talented Black children. He was a ferociously disciplined man who boasted that he never drank, smoked or engaged in lewd behaviour, and expected his children to live up to the same strict standards. His wife Ozie also had a background in teaching and both were accomplished pianists. The Professor, as Fletcher Snr's pupils had nicknamed him, bought a record player for the family at the end of World War One, but the only discs he'd allow in the house were hymns and spirituals like *Savior, Near the Cross* and *I Need Thee Every Hour*. Jazz and blues were condemned as trash – and sinful trash, at that.

Cuthbert's Black community accounted for about two-thirds of the town's 3,200 population during Fletcher Jr's childhood there, but his own family had little in common with the sharecroppers and labourers who made up most of that number. The Professor ensured that Fletcher – his oldest son – stuck to his piano lessons come what may. Whenever the boy rebelled, his father simply locked him a room with the piano and nothing else to do. "In the Henderson family, the piano stood for more than just respectability," Jeffrey Magree writes in his 2005 book on Henderson's career. "It also had to be used as a means of instilling the importance of education through discipline." [1]

Almost despite himself, Henderson started to get pretty good. He proved a bright lad in his school studies too, where his favourite subject was chemistry. In 1911, when he was 14, the family sent him off to Atlanta to join the university's College Prep Programme, where his classes included Latin, Greek, Algebra, American Literature, Maths and Science. He emerged in 1916 with the equivalent of a first-rate High School education and moved on to start a chemistry degree at the university itself. He paid for his tuition and his keep during the school year with janitorial work – just as Pace had done in his own time there – but was able to supplement this income with a summer job playing piano at a resort one of his lecturers owned in Massachusetts.

In 1919 he acted as the programme's named pianist in *The Open Door*, a big Atlanta University production telling the story of Black people in America. This was a big enough hit to go on to Savannah's Municipal Auditorium, again with Henderson as pianist, where there were over 300 people in the show's cast and so much demand for tickets that over a hundred would-be buyers were turned away. The Savannah show raised over $1,000 for the university (worth about $15,000 today) and gave Henderson his first taste of rapturous applause from a paying crowd.

He collected his chemistry degree in the Summer of 1920 – about the same time as Mamie Smith was recording *Crazy Blues* – and moved to New York where he hoped to continue his studies with a post-graduate chemistry course at Columbia. Turned down for a place there, he had to settle for some mundane lab work in downtown Manhattan, which lasted about a year.

Both Scott Fitzgerald's Jazz Age and the Harlem Renaissance were now well underway. For rich white New Yorkers, that meant wild parties like those in *The Great Gatsby*, and for African-Americans the huge cultural flowering which the influx of Black poets, novelists, playwrights, painters, dancers, singers, musicians and every kind of performer brought to Harlem itself. Pace would have recognized something of the freewheeling atmosphere from his time on Beale Street, but Harlem offered that heady thrill on a much larger scale. Every block between 110th Street and 155th Street buzzed with creative energy throughout the 1920s and Henderson, like Pace himself, arrived there just as it was all gathering speed. "What a Harlem it was!" Handy writes of his own time there in the same era. "Big old good-looking, easy-going, proud-walking Harlem!"

Once again music, though not yet his real passion, gave Henderson a useful way to earn some extra cash. His room-mate in Harlem was another pianist, who played in the resident orchestra on one of the nightclub boats which then sailed up and down the Hudson every evening. When he fell ill, he asked Henderson to substitute for him on the boat for a few nights, and that worked out fine. When the original pianist's illness stretched from days into weeks, the orchestra's leader, Fred "Deacon" Johnson, made Henderson his permanent replacement.

Johnson had also helped run the city's Clef Club, a popular hangout for New York's Black musicians, and knew Handy from his time there. Most likely it's this connection which let Henderson meet Handy for the first time, and led Handy to offer him a job as one of three new demonstration pianists at P&H. His pay would be $22.50 a week and Handy assigned him the ballads to play, while Georgia Gorham and Artemas Stevens handled jazz and blues. With the higher profile this job gave him, Henderson found doors opening throughout the city's musical community and many more gigs coming his way. Maybe chemistry wasn't where his future lay after all.

# Black Swan rising

*"The organization was the outgrowth of my
observation as President of the Pace & Handy
Music Co that phonograph companies were not
recording the voice of Negro singers and
musicians. [...] I therefore determined to form
my own company and make such recordings as
I believed would sell."*

**– Harry Pace in his 1939 letter to Roi Ottley.**

Pace was 36 years old as he started to put his plans for
Black Swan together, and that placed him right on the cusp
of a generational change in the music business. Handy, at
47, was too wedded to the old way of doing things to make
the leap of imagination which the shift from sheet music to
recorded discs demanded. Young men like Henderson, 23,
took records as a given and already saw sheet music sales
as the artefact of a bygone age. Pace could have jumped
either way as this chasm opened up beneath him, but he
was a shrewd enough businessman to make the right
choice. He couldn't have known it at the time, but the split
he was now contemplating would plunge Handy into the
darkest days of his life.

Looking around him in P&H's cramped offices,
Pace felt pretty confident he'd have his pick of its admin
staff when the time came. They were mostly in their

twenties, and no-one that age wanted to stay in the sheet music business for long. Henderson would be a good start among the musical talent he'd need, but Pace wanted William Grant Still too, and that might present more of a problem. Still, a versatile instrumentalist and a talented arranger, had joined P&H after a stint in Handy's orchestra, so that's where his oldest loyalties lay. Like Henderson, though, he was well under 30, and Pace hoped that would be enough to win him over. That kid Robeson might be useful too ... [1]

To understand the appeal Black Swan had for young African-Americans at the time, just imagine the twenty-something staff of a print newspaper today offered the chance to join a gleaming, hip new Silicon Valley start-up instead. The prospect of a new record label – let alone a Black-owned one – carried that kind of thrill for P&H's young staff as Pace prepared to launch, so it's no surprise they jumped aboard so keenly. It was a big adventure, and one that could hardly have been more exciting.

Pace, Henderson and Still quit P&H around the turn of the year, taking key staff from every level of the company with them. For Handy, the impact was devastating. The white record labels' campaign to boycott P&H's songs, combined with increased competition from those labels' in-house publishing operations was hitting the company's profits hard – and now this! "With Pace went a large number of our employees, persons especially trained for the requirements of our business and therefore hard to replace," he writes. "Still more confusion and anguish grew out of the fact that people did not generally know that I had no stake in Black Swan. Other companies must have felt that, by doing business with me as a publisher, they were helping a rival recording outfit."

Proof of that came shortly after Pace made his plans for Black Swan public, when a socialist newspaper called

*The Voice of the People* reported "two large white phonograph companies" had served notice on Handy that they would not be recording any more of his company's songs. But the planned boycott didn't stop with them. "Practically every one of the record companies read the announcement [of Black Swan's launch] and reached an understanding that no more songs published by Pace & Handy would be brought out on their records," the *VOTP* story continues. [2]

It meant nothing to these firms that Pace had already resigned from P&H and that the name on its charter now read Handy Brothers Music. The injustice of Handy being targeted in this way made Pace more defiant than ever. "The opposition of the white companies to the entry of a race organization into the phonograph record producing field makes me all the more determined," he told *VOTP's* reporter. "The public wants the kind of records I shall put out, and they will get them no matter who objects."

Robbed overnight not only of his partner's financial acumen but also of so many key employees, Handy's publishing business span towards trouble. It had been Pace, of course, who'd originally persuaded him to abandon his orchestra and switch to music publishing full-time, and also Pace who'd talked him into uprooting his family from Chicago to New York. Both these facts must have rankled with Handy, as must the news that even old friends like Still had decided to jump ship. Soon his health would desert him too, as an old dental implant became infected, spreading that infection to the rest of his face and leaving him blind for about four years. [3]

\*\*\*

Pace met with Dubois a few days before Christmas 1920 to outline his plans for the Pace Phonograph Corporation, inviting him a week later to join the new venture as both an investor and a member of its board. "I am converting much of my holdings in the South into cash to put into this enterprise and I think I can interest half a dozen other men who will put considerable sums into it," Pace assured him. [4]

He'd later claim that one crucial early investor was Bert Williams, the great Black vaudeville star, though it's worth noting that he delayed mentioning this until two weeks after Williams' death. "In the early months of this undertaking, when every dollar counted double, he put thousands into the making of Black Swan records," Pace said of Williams in a March 1922 *Crisis* ad. Not only that but, if he'd lived long enough to complete his existing Columbia contract, "he would have become, as he had promised, an exclusive Black Swan artist". [5]

DuBois accepted Pace's offer to join PPC's board and suggested they brand their records with the name Black Swan, a description originally used to promote the elegant Black concert singer Elizabeth Taylor Greenfield. Pace liked that idea a lot. By invoking Greenfield, he hoped to underline his own highbrow ambitions for the label. "He felt he had a mission to raise the taste of the African-American populace higher than the blues songs that were selling on other record labels," Berresford and Shor explain. "Much of what Pace termed 'cultural music' was the same light classics and sentimental fare which had dominated catalogues of the larger white-owned companies since the late 1890s." [6, 7]

Pace launched PPC with capital of $30,000 and a board of directors packed with Black America's most respected citizens. DuBois was there, along with John Nail (a renowned Harlem real estate pioneer), Matthew Boutte (a pharmacist and campaigner who'd been a captain in the wartime AEF) and Ethlynde's mother Viola Bibb.

The whole board shared both Pace's own disdain for popular music and his determination that the new firm must serve a wider purpose than record sales alone. Profitability was certainly important – no firm survives long without that – but no more so that PPC's role in creating new opportunities for everyone in the Black community and preventing the money they spent from leeching into white pockets. Black Swan was to be a Black-owned label, staffed by Black workers, recording Black artists making music for Black listeners to buy. Even when Pace came to drawing up plans for the label's own "Swanola" phonograph, he insisted it must be Black engineers who were trained to manufacture it. [8, 9]

African-American newspapers and magazines throughout the US gave PPC a warm welcome. *New York Age* called it one of the most important Black start-ups in the city, *Crisis* praised its "skilled management of guaranteed integrity" and Oklahoma City's *Black Dispatch* hailed it as "the first enterprise of its kind started by a Colored Corporation". That slight element of hedging – "of its kind" – may have been prompted by the fact that there had been one Black-owned record label in America already: a tiny Massachusetts mail-order operation called Broome Records which operated briefly in 1919 but collapsed again after issuing fewer than a dozen sides. The difference the papers recognized in Black Swan was that it promised to operate on a truly national scale and to achieve a level of success that a minnow like Broome could never have hoped for. [10, 11]

Gratifying as all this launch publicity was, Pace still faced many practical problems before he could get the company's production underway. At the top of his list was finding a recording studio and a pressing plant prepared to accept his business – a search which the white record labels were determined to frustrate in every way they could. Whenever Pace approached one of them about leasing excess capacity at their own pressing plants, they turned him away flat. He thought he'd found the answer when the tiny Operaphone label went bust at the beginning of 1921, leaving its factory and studio buildings in Long Island City up for grabs at a bargain price. Located just across the East River from PPC's Manhattan HQ, that would have been a wonderfully convenient and cost-saving location for Black Swan to use.

Pace's white rivals thought so too and stepped in to ensure his bid was rejected. "They purchased this plant from its then owners and sold it to the Remington concern in order to shut off Mr Pace's facilities for manufacturing," the *Richmond Planet* later reported. The plant ended up making discs for Remington's Olympic label instead which, just like Operaphone before it, failed to make the place pay. John Fletcher, Operaphone's founder, stayed on as part of the deal – and we'll be meeting him again later.
(12)

Pace gives these struggles just two dispassionate sentences in his letter to Ottley, saying only that it took him a long time to find a pressing plant because "all of the bigger record companies refused to press records for outsiders". It's impossible to say how much of that refusal was motivated by simple racism on the white companies' part and how much by their fear of the strong new competition they expected Black Swan would bring. The fact that Pace was eventually forced to go all the way to Port Washington in Wisconsin to get his discs pressed does suggest a co-ordinated campaign against him, however – and a pretty extensive one at that.

The Port Washington plant Pace signed with belonged to the Wisconsin Chair Company, which also used it to manufacture discs for its own Paramount Records subsidiary. WCC had got into the music business in 1917, expanding its core furniture business first to make Paramount-branded phonographs and then adding the discs themselves. It had another subsidiary called New York Recording Laboratories, whose Manhattan studio was made available for Black Swan to rent as part of the same agreement. Signing this deal meant Pace would have to ship all his master discs over 700 miles before manufacturing could even begin, but what other choice did he have?

This time, the major white-owned labels' bosses allowed it all to go through, chuckling over their speakeasy gin at the extra costs and delays Black Swan would now have to overcome.

*** 

Operating from an office in Pace's basement and the rented NYRL studio, Black Swan geared up for its first releases with Still writing arrangements and Henderson as recording manager. Pace was seldom seen in the studio, leaving Henderson in charge there to choose the musicians needed for each recording and rehearse them before the sessions began. "Harry Pace's role was that of an executive," Still later recalled. "[He] would oversee the musical progress, listen to the singers and pass on the choice of music for recordings. Everything had to come up for his final judgement." The company's first recording sessions began in February, interspersed with studio tests for any promising nightclub singers who Henderson thought might be worth signing. There was one particular prospect whose test he wanted Pace to witness for himself – and her name was Bessie Smith. [13]

Smith had been building a formidable reputation for herself in dive bars and jazz clubs throughout the South since 1913, but she'd not yet made a record. Her big, earthy bellow of a voice and boisterous personality made her just the sort of Black performer who Pace considered too crude for words, but Henderson clearly thought she had something, so he obediently trotted along to the studio to hear her audition. All went well till Smith broke off part way through one of her songs and announced she needed to spit. That was all Pace needed to reject her there and then, declaring the audition over and leaving Smith to stalk out and sign with Columbia instead. Within a couple of years, she'd be selling boatloads of records for them and generating a flood of cash that could so easily have gone to Black Swan instead. Handy took great delight in telling this story against his old partner for years to come, restoring his hurt pride with a chuckle at just how much money Pace's prissy ways had cost the label. [14]

Shaking off the Smith encounter, Pace turned his attention to marketing and distribution. Right from the beginning, he wanted to ensure every Black Swan ad and record sleeve stressed the label's unique mission. "The only phonograph company owned and controlled by colored people," one slogan declared. "The only records using exclusively Negro voices and musicians," added another. At a time when blues discs were routinely promoted with bug-eyed, big-lipped racial caricatures, Black Swan's sleeves stood out for their dignified blocks of type flagging up the label's Black ownership and the high level of craftsmanship its engineers employed: "The only records made entirely by colored people"; "A good record of Merit and Quality"; "Compares favorably with those produced by any other company". [15]

Distribution was a tougher nut to crack. With no established network willing to take him on, and few white retailers who'd deal with him either, Pace was forced to start from scratch. He ran press ads throughout the US to recruit Black salesmen willing to tout his records door-to-door or set up as a small regional wholesaler in their own right. "Go into business for yourself," the ads declared. "Sell Black Swan Records. Agents and Dealers Wanted Everywhere." These ads pulled in a huge and enthusiastic response from Black neighbourhoods all over America. Already, there was great goodwill for Pace's enterprise, and everyone wanted to do their bit in helping get its records in front of potential buyers. Pullman porters would slip a box or two of Black Swan records on board their trains to drop off at rural stops. Where no traditional outlets were available, Black barber shops, pool halls and drinking joints agreed to stock the discs instead. Newsboys hawked them on their rounds. [16, 17]

Black Swan's first three discs, released in May 1921, were *At Dawning* by the soprano Revella Hughes, *For All Eternity* by baritone Carroll Clark and *Blind Man's Blues* by Katie Crippen. The first two were examples of the self-consciously "improving" material which the genteel Pace hoped would elevate his people's tastes, but the Crippen record aimed squarely at sales. Mamie Smith's success a year earlier had proved beyond doubt that there was a lot of money to be made from blues records, and Pace knew better than to argue with that.

Henderson was a little disappointed with the Crippen record, feeling it could have been given a bolder, more aggressive blues treatment, but it sold well enough to prompt competing cover versions from both Mary Stafford at Columbia and Okeh's Sara Martin. No-one was rushing out covers of Hughes' or Clark's songs, which should have given Pace an early hint Black Swan might not end up developing in quite the way he'd hoped. He wasn't ready to give up his highbrow ambitions just yet, but it was already clear that blues was going to be crucial to the company's survival. "We have had to give people what many of them wanted in order to get them to want what we wanted them to want," Pace admitted in a 1921 speech to the National Association of Negro Musicians. But offering blues alone, he added, could never be enough:

> *"I believe we want every kind music other people want, and it behooves some of us to undertake the job of elevating the musical taste of the race. Black Swan Records are trying to do their part. [...] If, through lack of patronage for our higher-class numbers we are compelled to record only blues and ragtime, the public critics and the white companies will join in a chorus of 'I told you so'. The dictum will go forth that Negroes will not buy good music, and the chance of our artist ever recording his voice for any white organization will fade into the realm of chances lost and not to be regained."*

The hurdles Pace had to overcome just to get Black Swan started, coupled with the high standards he insisted on for everything it made, inflated every aspect of the firm's production costs, making it necessary for Pace to price his records at $1 instead of the 85 cents his competitors charged. Within a couple of weeks, it was clear this price differential was undermining sales, which totaled only $674.64 for the whole of Black Swan's first month. Pace had no choice but to match his competitors' price after all, which left the profit he could extract from each disc looking perilously thin. [18]

Pace knew all his white-owned rivals were already drawing up plans to launch their own specialist imprints for Black artists – known as "race records" imprints – which aimed to avoid trouble from distributors by bundling all the company's Black singers and musicians into a corral of their own. Not everyone who bought those imprints' discs would be Black, but that was definitely the core market they had in mind. Giants like Columbia and Victor would be targeting Pace's customers very soon – and doing so with an ad spend that dwarfed his own. Unless something turned up soon, Black Swan might not survive long enough to celebrate its first birthday.

*Ethel Waters. Art by Karl Stevens.*

## Sweet Mama Stringbean

*"Clifton Street, located in the old Bloody Eighth ward, lay in the heart of the red-light district. [...] I was not yet six years old when we moved there, and seven when we left, but I had one hell of a time for myself in that plague spot of vice and crime. I came to know well the street whores, the ladies in the sporting houses, their pimps, the pickpockets, shoplifters and other thieves who lived all around us. I played with the thieves' children and the sporting women's trick babies.'*

**– Ethel Waters in her 1950 autobiography**
***His Eye is on the Sparrow.***

Ethel Waters had the roughest start in life it's possible to imagine. Her mother was a Black teenager called Louise Anderson, who was just 13 years old when she gave birth to Ethel in Chester, Pennsylvania, on October 31, 1900. The father was John Waters, a mixed-race pianist who knew Louise's family and often visited the tumbledown shack she shared with her mother Sally and Sally's other three children: Viola, Charlie and Edith. Vi was the oldest, and often left in charge of the other kids when Sally was out at work. "She could sing beautifully, like all the women in my family," Ethel writes. "But she had an insane temper."

Maybe it's that temper which explains what Vi did one night in January 1900. Maybe Louise had annoyed her in some way and she wanted revenge. Here's Ethel again:

*"There was a saying used then when anyone wanted to ask if a girl was a virgin. They would say, 'Is she broke in yet?' One day John Waters asked Vi, 'Is Louise broke in yet?' [...] Vi told him to come round on a day when she was sure my grandmother wouldn't be home. So John Waters, my father, came back one day and forced my mother to submit to him. She tried to fight him, but he raped her, holding a knife. She was only twelve and didn't know what it was all about, but she had to give in to him. And that is how I was conceived."* [1]

John Waters wanted no part of raising or supporting his daughter. Louise's own mother, Sally, was so incensed by what he'd done that she chased him off whenever he dared get within 100 yards of the child – or of Louise either, for that matter. Three years later, he was fatally poisoned by a jealous woman, and Ethel was led up to see him in his coffin at the funeral. She'd never knowingly set eyes on her father till that day.

Louise was too young to care for a kid alone, so Sally, Viola, Edith and Sally's sister Ida all mucked in too. Louise herself was glad enough to leave most of the childcare to them, watching from the sidelines as Ethel was shuffled round from one hard-pressed relative to the next. It was a childhood of chaotic poverty, enmeshed in petty crime and offering little of the secure affection every child craves. "I never was coddled or liked or understood by my family," Ethel confides in her book. 'I never felt I belonged." [2]

The one saving grace of this ragged upbringing was that the boozy Viola and Edith both loved to sing, filling their niece's head with songs like *I Don't Want to Play in Your Yard*, *There'll Come a Time* and *The Volunteer Organist*. The best of these songs were short stories set to music, telling of childhood friendships lost and regained, or tattered vagrants with an unexpected talent to reveal. They became Ethel's fairy tales, holding her just as rapt with their own twists and turns as fables of princes and diamond slippers might have done for more fortunate children. Her own voice would one day combine the sweet tones of Viola's singing with the sharp clarity of Edith's, but her first lesson from them was how to inhabit a song and make listeners yearn to know what happened next. "It was always the story told in the song that enchanted me," she recalls. "I'd ask one of them 'Tell me a story,' and they'd sing it."

When Ethel was five, Sally found some new accommodation in Philadelphia's notorious eighth ward. It was only a three-room shanty in an alleyway off Clifton Street, but it provided just enough space for the family to reunite under one roof after a spell apart. It was here, in the Bloody Eighth, that Ethel played her first gig – a kids' show for worshippers at Sally's church - and also where she started running with one of the area's child gangs. She learnt to shoplift, and to earn a few cents for herself as a look-out for the local brothel. Some nights, when the weather was good, she'd sleep out on a hot air grate rather than return to the crowded apartment. At eight, she discovered the vaudeville shows that filled South Street's tiny storefront theatres, sneaking into their 10 cent auditoriums to watch her favourite performers again and again. When the owners finally threw her out, she'd run back to Viola and Edith to perform the songs she'd memorized there: songs like *Lovie Joe* and *Barber Shop Chord*. [3]

By the time Ethel was 13, her body had developed enough for the lads she met at neighbourhood dances to start taking notice. The most persistent was a 23-year-old steel worker called Merritt Purnsley who everyone knew as "Buddy". Ethel liked his looks well enough, but all her instincts screamed this man was not to be trusted. However hard he tried to seduce her, she turned him away. Finally – realizing perhaps that there was no other way to get what he wanted – he proposed marriage. She tried to fob him off by saying she couldn't possibly marry him unless he got Louise's permission first. "I just wanted to get rid of him and counted on my mother to refuse, for she knew well what I thought of Buddy," she writes. "But when he asked her about it, she double-crossed me by saying 'Yes, you can marry my Ethel'. I felt betrayed and thought she'd agreed only because marrying me off to Buddy was an easy way of eliminating me as a problem."

Purnsley had her trapped now. She was too young to marry legally in Pennsylvania, but he took care of that by obtaining a fraudulent licence giving her age as 18. Ethel was heartbroken, not just at how casually Louise had discarded her, but also at the fact that Sally was now too frail and ill to attend the wedding. The ceremony itself was a loveless, perfunctory affair, and that night's consummation as brutal as Ethel had feared. Louise threw a little cheap furniture their way and they were left to get on with it.

Ethel returned to school for a few months, completing sixth grade in June 1914, then found work. She did her best not to anger the foul-tempered Purnsley, but it was all in vain. Soon, he'd begun an affair with another woman, transferring his guilt at this betrayal into baseless allegations against Ethel's own fidelity, and beating her whenever she refused to knuckle under to his constant bullying. Slowly, her initial fear of this vile man hardened into contempt. She walked out after less than a year, a huge weight lifting from her shoulders as she left. "That husband of mine, who'd once been so terrifying, had become just another termite to me," she writes. "At thirteen I was married, and at fourteen I was separated and on my own. I had a certain amount of battle cry in me."

\*\*\*

Sally was dead by the time Waters escaped and the family already dispersed, so there was no going back to her old life. She got a job in a Philadelphia hotel instead, first as one of its dishwashers and then graduating to chambermaid. It didn't pay much, so she had to take in laundry from the guests too, but who cared about that when the combined income meant she was independent at last? Day after day, she'd hurry through cleaning each room to buy herself a few minutes of freedom in front of its full-length mirror, crooning quietly to her own reflection and practicing the stage moves she remembered from South Street. This was her life now.

Her first break came at a 1917 Halloween party in Jack's Rathskeller, a saloon on the corner of Juniper and South streets used by the small-time performers and impresarios who worked the storefront theatres nearby. Egged on by one of her friends, Waters stepped on to the tiny stage and sang a sentimental wartime ballad called *When You're a Long, Long Way from Home*. "The crowd liked my rich, young voice, and I had to give two or three encores," she writes. "Among the professionals there were Braxton & Nugent, who had a small vaudeville unit. They said if I would work on the stage with them, they could get me ten dollars a week." The only snag was her age: still just 17, she was too young for the duo to take her on without a convenient lie in place to protect themselves from the law. "The two vaudevillians talked it over with my mother," Waters writes. "They told her they could get me two weeks down [at the Lincoln Theatre] in Baltimore if she would only sign a paper swearing I was twenty-one. She signed without any arguments." [4]

Waters began preparing for the Baltimore show straight away, buying herself a thrift shop gown to wear onstage and working out which songs to perform. There was one particular number she wanted to include, a song she'd once heard a female impersonator called Charles Anderson do but, as yet, no-one else. That song was *St Louis Blues*.

Braxton & Nugent explained that the song's copyright holders – Pace & Handy, of course – had slapped some restrictions on this song, meaning that anyone but Handy who wanted to perform it had to get the company's written permission first. Anderson may have had a low enough profile to risk flouting this rule, but their own show did not. It was a ballsy move for a singer as young and utterly unknown as Waters to make, but she figured she had nothing to lose and wrote to P&H anyway. "They answered my letter by granting me permission," she writes, still sounding like she can't believe her luck. "That was how I, a seventeen-year-old novice, became the first woman – and the second person – ever to professionally sing that song."

Nabbing one of the great WC Handy's best songs in this way was a real coup, so Braxton and Nugent were determined to make the most of its staging at the Lincoln. Waters and Nugent would walk on stage, playing a couple already locked in an angry row. Nugent then stormed off, announcing he was going to see his other girl, leaving Waters on stage alone in a rocking chair. "I'd sit there, rocking sadly and slowly," she writes. "Then I would sing *St Louis Blues*, but very softly. It was the first time that kind of Negro audience ever let my kind of low singing get by.

You could have heard a pin drop in that rough, rowdy audience out front. [...] That first time, when I finished singing *St Louis Blues*, the money fell like rain on the stage. Nugent had to come on to get me off or I would have been sitting there yet."

Waters' trademark style was already starting to emerge. Many of the Black women performing blues at this time would shout their lyrics as much as sing them, relying on sheer volume to get the power of the song across. Waters preferred to croon, using her sharp diction to draw the audience into the story she was telling and demanding they listen till that story was done. "She was a jazz singer," the clarinetist Garvin Bushell later explained. "She syncopated. Her style was influenced by the horns she'd heard and by church singing. She literally sang with a smile, which made her voice sound wide and broad." Andrea Barnet makes a similar point in her 2004 book *All-Night Party*. "She had the sexual swagger of singers like Bessie Smith and Ma Rainey, yet her voice was softer," she says of Waters. "Ethel's style was crisp and urbane, more northern." [5, 6]

Just a few weeks earlier, Waters had been terrified at the prospect of taking on the Lincoln Theatre shows, but now her confidence was growing fast. By the time the Lincoln run was finished, she'd concluded that Braxton and Nugent were taking more than their fair share of both the extra ticket revenue she brought in and of the cash tips flooding the stage every time she sang. She completed the final night, accused the startled pair of cheating her and, when they refused to budge, quit the troupe. The Hill Sisters, another act on B&N's Lincoln Theatre bill, followed her – presumably because they were sick of getting the same treatment. Jo and Maggie Hill then formed a trio with Waters and the three women began touring in their own right. That worked fine for a while, but the Hills got jealous when promotors started singling out Waters and her *St Louise Blue* performance in all in all their billing. Their bond as sisters made it easy to freeze her out backstage. When Maggie quit, Waters worked briefly with Jo, supposedly as a duo, but knowing full well it was her the audience really wanted to see. She was a beautiful young woman now – albeit rather a lanky one – and found her fans had given her an affectionate nickname: Sweet Mama Stringbean. [7]

It was time to go solo. After a spell with a travelling tent show, Waters shipped up in Atlanta to play a few nights' shows at a Decatur Street theatre where Bessie Smith was topping the bill. Waters was in her late teens now, and her reputation had grown to a point where even the empress of Southern blues clearly viewed her as a threat. When Smith discovered who would be supporting her at the Decatur Street gigs, she told the club's owners that Waters must not be allowed to include any blues in her set. They had no choice but to go along, and passed news of the embargo on to Waters, who agreed to stick by it. She had plenty of ballads in her repertoire and had begun to include a little shimmy dancing in the act which she knew always went down well. If Smith wanted her to skip the blues numbers for a few nights, that was fine.

The audience had other ideas. "When I went on I sang *I Want to be Somebody's Baby Doll So I Can Get My Lovin' All the Time*," Waters writes. "Before I could finish this number, the people out front started howling 'Blues! Blues! Come on, Stringbean, we want your blues!' The two-man orchestra struck up Bessie's music and kept it up through three refrains while the audience, feeling cheated, kept yelling 'We want Stringbean and her blues!'"

The theatre's owner knocked nervously at Smith's dressing room door in the break before the second show and told her he couldn't risk provoking that kind of audience protest again: he was going to have to let Waters sing her blues stuff after all. "There was quite a stormy discussion about this, and you could hear Bessie yelling things about 'these Northern bitches'," Waters writes. "[But she] agreed that, after I took two or three bows for my first song, I should, if the crowd still insisted, sing *St Louis Blues*. And each audience did insist." When the final night at Decatur Street was done, Smith called her over to offer an olive branch: "You ain't so bad," Waters reports her saying. "It's only that I never dreamed anyone would be able to do this to me in my own territory and with my own people." [8]

\*\*\*

Waters' progress after the Atlanta gigs was stopped dead by a 1918 car accident which left her too injured to travel. Live performances were then the only way a singer could earn money, so she was forced to put her career on hold while she recuperated at home in Philadelphia. She was washing dishes in an automat there to make ends meet when Joe Bright, a New York promoter, persuaded her she was ready to return to the stage. He booked her two weeks at the Lincoln Theatre in Handy's "good-looking, easy-going, proud-walking Harlem", and Waters liked it so much there she decided to stay. When the Lincoln Theatre run was over, one of its dancers put her in touch with the owners of a Harlem nightclub called Edmond's Cellar, whose owner – a former boxer - agreed to give her slot on the bill. The pay was $2 a night, same as everyone else there got, plus a share of the communal tips jar. [9]

Known fondly to its regulars as "The Bucket of Blood", Edmonds was a rough old joint, played either by those just starting their climb up the showbiz ladder or those about to topple off its bottom rung. Waters wasn't quite sure which category she belonged in at that moment, but work was work and the job let her stay on in Harlem rather than returning to Philadelphia. Soon, she was gigging at Edmond's almost every night, edging up her wage a little with each new negotiation, and beginning to think of this basement dive as a second home. Here's her description of its décor and clientele:

*"Edmond's was a small place and seated between 150 and 200 people, who sat at tables jammed close together around a handkerchief-size dance floor. It had a very low ceiling which Edmond Johnson had decorated with paper chrysanthemums and streamers. The walls were covered with fading photographs of old-time fighters and Negro entertainers. Edmond was very proud of his decorations, particularly the chrysanthemums."*

*"I am no stoolie, but I don't think it can hurt anybody if I say that there were many junkies, gamblers and thieves down in that cellar at all times. We'd report at nine o'clock at night and sometimes not get out of there until eight, or even ten next morning. We always had to wait for our turn to go on. But then we could stay out on that floor as long as we liked if the tips kept coming in."* [10]

It was around this time that Waters began pursuing a talented Alhambra Theatre dancer called Ethel Williams, described in one review as having "the form of a Venus and the eyes of a devil". Ever since her time with the Hill Sisters – and perhaps before that too – Waters had been just as happy to sleep with women as with men. Partly, this came through spending so much of her life on the road, as Donald Bogle explains in his 2011 biography of Waters.

"On the road, some grew lonely," he writes. "Same-sex relationships flourished for some women and at times were even commonplace. 'Often, we girls would share a room because of the cost,' entertainer Maude Russell once told an interviewer. 'In those days, men only wanted what they wanted, they didn't care about pleasing a girl. Girls needed tenderness, so we had girl friendships, the famous lady lovers.'" (11, 12, 13)

Waters certainly hadn't seen much tenderness from the men in her life and didn't much seem to care if people found out her new partner was a woman. The pair began sharing an apartment together and the besotted Waters gave up part of her own pay at Edmond's to secure Williams a job there. "They were known as The Two Ethels," their contemporary Elisabeth Welch later recalled. "It was scandalous for two women to live together as a couple. The other Ethel was light-skinned, skinny and red-haired. [...] Most people knew that they were lovers and we heard that they sometimes argued in public." These rows were usually triggered by the jealous Waters accusing Williams of chasing some other woman, but instead of thrashing out their disagreements at home, they did so on Harlem's crowded sidewalks. "They used to fight up and down Seventh Avenue," Mabel Hampton, another singer working at the same time, recalled. "Men couldn't do nothing 'cause they were good. They were money-makers, you know?" (14, 15)

Soon, this volatile couple was part of the local entertainment. One night, Waters returned from the lady's room in a club where she'd been watching Williams dance to find a drunken white man rifling through her handbag and decked him with a single punch. This was the era of Jack Johnson, the first Black heavyweight champion, and the other drinkers watching that night dubbed Waters "Miss Johnson" to reflect her punch's impressive power. Even the resident gangsters – some with a murder or two to their credit – would playfully beg her not to hit them whenever she looked displeased. [16]

With her slot at Edmond's now secure and her girlfriend installed on the bill there too, Waters' life and career were firmly back on track. All she needed now was a record deal.

# Their first big hit

*"What surprised everyone about* Down Home Blues *was the sales – it just went berserk. From doing $700 a month, they were turning over $20,000 a month as soon as this record was issued. And it pointed most emphatically to Pace the direction in which Black Swan should have been going. There's enough life and excitement and vibrancy in that record to make you want to listen to it again and again."*

**- Mark Berresford, speaking to the author in 2007.**

Waters' first recording session was on March 21, 1921, when a tiny New York label called Cardinal hired her to record *New York Glide* and *At the New Jump Steady Ball.* The resulting disc sank without trace, but a month later she found herself back in a studio again – this time for Black Swan. Quite how she came to hook up with Pace's label is hotly disputed, with everyone involved telling a different story. This was a major coup for Black Swan and Waters alike, which means everyone's keen to cast themselves as the one who made it possible.

Fletcher Henderson's account is the shortest, so let's start with him. This is from a *Jazz Monthly* interview published in 1957:

*"I was walking along 135th Street in Harlem one night and there, in a basement, singing with all her heart was Ethel. I had her come down and cut four sides, of which two –* Down Home Blues *and* Oh Daddy *– became such hits that we were made."* [1]

He doesn't mention the club's name, but its address and basement location both suggest Edmond's. Pace has a different version, this one given in his 1939 letter to Roi Ottley:

*"While in Atlantic City, I went to a cabaret on the West Side at the invitation of a mutual friend, who stated that there was a girl there singing with a peculiar voice that he thought I might use. I heard this girl and I invited her over to my table to talk about coming to New York to make a recording.*

*"She very brusquely refused, but at the same time I saw that she was interested, and I told her that I would send her a ticket to New York on the next Wednesday. I did send such a ticket and she came to New York and made two records,* Down Home Blues *and* Oh Daddy. *This girl was Ethel Waters, and the records were enormously successful."*

That "very brusquely" certainly sounds like Waters. But when she tells the story herself, Atlantic City doesn't figure at all:

*"The same talent scout who dug me up for Cardinal worked for other record companies. After catching my*

*act at Edmond's a second time, he asked if I would care to make some records for Black Swan, a new company just started by Harry H Pace and WC Handy [sic], the two grand old men of Negro music.* [2]

*"The Black Swan office was in the home of one of the owners. The day I went there I found Fletcher Henderson sitting behind a desk looking very prissy and important. [...] There was much discussion of whether I should sing popular or 'cultural' numbers. They finally decided on popular and I asked one hundred dollars for making the record. I was still getting only thirty-five dollars a week and tips, so one hundred dollars seemed quite a lump sum to me.* [3]

*"Mr Pace paid me the one hundred dollars, and that first Black Swan record I made had* Down Home Blues *on one side and* Oh Daddy *on the other. It proved a great success and a best seller among both white and colored, and it got Black Swan out of the red."*


Whatever the truth of the matter, the end result was the same: Waters turned up at Black Swan's Manhattan studio ready to record. The studio was a small room with a serving hatch cut into one wall, where engineers placed a large recording horn like the one seen in His Master's Voice ads. There were no microphones in those days, so everyone sang and played into the horn, its attached needle cutting their music directly on to a spinning wax master disc in the next room. This produced a long, curly shaving of discarded wax, which one of the engineers would periodically sweep to the floor. The master disc's turntable was driven by a weight-and-pulley arrangement to keep its speed steady, which meant no take could last longer than the three-and-a-half minutes or so it took that weight to reach the ground.

Alberta Hunter, who'd record for Black Swan in this same room just a few weeks after Waters, later spoke of the great care all the label's technicians took to ensure they got a good recording. Sound had to be mixed live on the floor, the balance of one instrument against another governed purely by how close each was to the horn that captured its sound. Some instruments, such as drums, had to be banned altogether, or they'd simply have drowned out everything around them. Photographs from the time show musicians crammed into every corner of a studio's very limited space, some perched precariously on tables or other improvised platforms to project sound over their colleagues' heads. "Since we couldn't use a bass drum or a bass, the rhythm tended to get ragged," Bushell recalled of one Black Swan session. "Also, we'd be in awkward positions and scattered all over the place, which made it hard to keep together. But we had good musicians who were concerned about what they were playing."

Waters' voice came as a breath of fresh air to Pace – particularly after his run-in with Bessie Smith a few weeks earlier. Her light, sweet tones were a world away from Smith's earthy growl, and yet she managed to make the blues numbers in her repertoire work just as well as the more innocent ballads. Smith clearly hadn't been what he was looking for, and Katie Crippen wasn't really to his liking either, but Waters offered an appealing compromise between the records he really wanted to release and those which people might actually buy. He didn't know it yet, but the day Waters walked into that studio in the Spring of 1921 was the day Black Swan struck gold.

Driven along by a bluesy, belching trombone, *Down Home Blues* is narrated by a woman whose much-loved man has just deserted her. Plunged into utter despair, she has no choice but to board the next train back down South, returning to the poverty she thought she'd finally left behind. There's a tasty little trumpet solo before the final verse, then everyone kicks it up a notch for their final blast through to the finish line. Even with the music behind her at its loudest, Waters has no difficulty making herself heard and – just as important – understood. And yet she never neglects to *sing* rather than merely bellow. Whether she's softly confiding her private pain to the listener ("he broke my heart") or belting out a moment's defiance ("no use in grieving"), she sells every line and makes it real. On a more trivial note, the song's lyrics also allow her to give that future blues cliche "woke up this morning" what may well be its first appearance on disc.

***

*Down Home Blues* was not only Black Swan's first big seller, but also the disc that rescued the company's finances. Pace claims in his letter to Ottley that it sold 500,000 copies in its first six months – a figure which everyone agrees is a vast exaggeration – but even the more probable total of around 120,000 is impressive enough. By the standards of the day, sales of 100,000 marked a major hit, and the effect of this on Black Swan's income was dramatic. The same *New York Age* story which gives us that $674.64 figure for the label's February 1921 sales reports December's equivalent figure at $20,467.82 – a thirty-fold increase. Sales for the eleven months to January 1, 1922, it adds, totaled $104,628.74, almost all of which came in the period after *Down Home Blues'* release. When Pace came to prepare Black Swan's accounts for calendar 1921, he listed a net profit of $10,856.78, which would be worth close to $160,000 today. [4, 5]

He responded to the first signs of this new success by replacing Waters' initial one-off payment with a year's contract designed to lock her in as an exclusive Black Swan artist. "The next month, I had her make two other records and thereafter, for a long, time, she made a record a month," he tells Ottley. "But none of them ever measured up to the *Down Home Blues* record. I then began to invite other well-known singers and performers and, within a year, I was issuing about 12 records a month and selling them in every state in the United States, and in a good many foreign countries." [6]

The label had a workforce of 30 people now, far too many to accommodate in Pace's home basement, so he bought a three-storey building on 135th and Seventh to become its new HQ, fitting out the ground floor as the shipping department and the two above as offices. In October 1921, he released four more Ethel Waters sides, including the future jazz classic *There'll Be Some Changes Made*, which she was the first person to record. A week later, the *Chicago Defender* reported Black Swan was now shipping 2,500 discs a day and had recruited over 1,000 dealers and agents throughout the country to help distribute them. [7]

Top priority now was to get Waters heard by as many people as possible and see just how many records she night be able to sell if the label put a major push behind her. Music radio was more or less unknown in the US at this time, so the answer Pace hit on was to dispatch his biggest star on a ground-breaking national tour. Her backing band would be the label's studio orchestra, led by Henderson, and renamed Ethel Waters' Jazz Masters for the tour's duration. Also in the eight-strong band were Gus Aiken (cornet), Bud Aiken (trombone), Garvin Bushell (clarinet), Joe Elder, saxophone), Charlie Jackson (violin), Bill "DC" (baritone saxophone) and Raymond Green (drums/xylophone). Waters took a little persuading to give up her steady gig at Edmond's for such an extended trip, but eventually agreed. [8, 9]

Pace conceived the tour as a full revue show, with Waters and the band headlining every night and a full variety bill in support. Waters wanted her girlfriend along for the trip, so she insisted that Williams and her dance partner be given a regular spot just before the Jazz Masters came on. All the other acts would be booked locally, drawing on the best Black comedians, acrobats and hoofers each town had to offer. The outfit in full – not just Ethel and the band but everyone else as well – would be known as the Black Swan Troubadours.

Henderson had no fears about his abilities as either pianist or bandleader, but felt he could not possibly leave New York for such a scandalous project as a blues tour without getting his dictatorial father's permission first. The Professor insisted he must meet Waters before giving his verdict. Would she be a suitably respectable companion for his son, or was she the sort of low type who'd drag him into the gutter of 12-bar degradation? We can get a glimpse of Henderson Senior's fears for his son in a short story he wrote just a few months after the tour proposal came up. This featured Silas, a young man who leaves the family farm for a job in the big city and ends up warning the sinners he meets there against card-playing, drinking and dancing "because you just can't do them things and be like Jesus wants you to be". [10]

Waters was convinced her pianist had doubts of his own – though there it seems to be his social standing rather than his soul that was the worry. "Fletcher wasn't sure it would be dignified enough for him, a college student studying chemistry, to be the piano player for a girl who sang blues in a cellar," she writes. "Remember those class distinctions in Harlem, which had its Park Avenue and its Tenth Avenue. That was me then, low-down Tenth Avenue." Henderson begged Waters to be on her best behaviour and then nervously invited his family up from Georgia to New York so they could look her over. She must surely have teased him mercilessly about being a grown man who still needed his daddy's permission to leave town, but when the time came she turned her full stage charm on the old man and won the whole family over with ease. "They fell in love with me at first sight," she says with some satisfaction.

The showbiz circuit, like everything else in 1920s America, was segregated, so Pace booked the tour's venues through the Theatre Owners' Booking Association, which represented about 80 Black-owned theatres throughout the US. Here's Bushell on how the live music industry worked in those days:

> *"There were Negro theaters all over the South and Midwest. Many were very small nickelodeons. They were often dirty, with dressing rooms in the cellar. [...] The Negro theaters remained because Negroes couldn't go to white theaters in those towns. When I came to New York, there was only one theater in Harlem where I could sit downstairs, and that was the Lafayette. Wherever there were whites, we couldn't sit downstairs till 1927. That made us bitter. In some white theaters a Negro could go through the alley, up five or six flights and sit in the gallery above the balcony. But in those theaters, you didn't see many Negro entertainers, and no Negro singers."* [11]

These high-altitude galleries were known as "the crows' nest", and comprised the worst seats in the whole house, placing Black patrons as far from the stage as it was possible to get. Black theatres gave African-Americans a much better view, but most were starved of cash, and forced to operate with only the most basic facilities. TOBA itself couldn't afford many frills either, and offered its touring artists so few comforts that its initials were wryly said to stand for "Tough On Black Asses". Whatever else the Troubadours could expect on the tour, glamour and luxury were out. [12]

Some of the larger Black-owned theatres might occasionally set aside a section for white patrons if the night's bill justified it – though seldom in such a demeaning position as the crows' nest - but primarily the Troubadours' tour was to be a Black show playing to a Black audience. Tours on the scale Pace envisaged were a new thing in 1921, so the logistics must have been pretty daunting, but he pressed on. By the time he was done, they had shows booked in well over 50 towns and cities all over the US, covering 20 states in all. Finally, everything was in place and, in November 1921, the Black Swan Troubadours' core acts left New York for an eight-month stint on the road

# Life on the road

> *"We made about $50 a week, I guess. Conditions of traveling didn't bother us too much. If you had to walk the streets all night or sleep in a church, you did it. Sometimes we couldn't get a room and we'd have to call up the black preacher. [...] Accommodations in Negro neighborhoods could be lousy – with bad food and lots of bedbugs. But being young, we didn't care. We were having a ball on the road."*
>
> **- Garvin Bushell in his 1988 book *Jazz From the Beginning*.**

The Troubadours began their tour with a show in Washington DC on November 17, 1921. There's a lot to say about the adventures they had at each stop along the way, so I'm going to break this chapter down into a city-by-city account. [1]

**Washington DC, Nov 17, 1921.**

Opening night of the tour.

**Philadelphia: Gibson's Standard Theatre, Nov 21-27.**

Pace pulled off something of a coup by persuading Jack Johnson, the former heavyweight champion, to join the show for its week's run in Philadelphia. This was the man who'd not only beaten every challenger white America could throw at him in the ring, but also took great pleasure in ramming that point home to infuriated racists. Everywhere he went, Johnson wore expensive suits, drove the best cars and – most provocatively of all – always took care to have a beautiful white girlfriend on his arm. As the Black Swan tour began, he'd just been released from Leavenworth prison after serving ten months on a trumped-up miscegenation charge and was ready to reclaim his standing as the biggest Black celebrity in America. [2]

Just by being there, Johnson guaranteed every night in Philadelphia was sold out. For most of the audience, it was enough simply to be in the same room as a Black man who'd navigated white America with such uncompromising aplomb. "People just wanted to look at him," Bushell recalls.

Alongside Johnson on the bill in Philadelphia were Waters, Williams and the band, plus Sandy Burns, a well-known Black comedian, the tenor singer Slick White, a piano duo called Baker & Baker and two pairs of song-and-dance partners who mixed cross-talk routines with their own musical numbers. When Johnson's slot came round each night, he'd talk about his fight career from the stage for a while, demonstrate a little shadow boxing and then join Burns in a mock sparring match which had the *Chicago Defender's* man in fits. "The funniest bit pulled off here in many moons was a burlesque fight between Jack Johnson and Sandy Burns," he told his readers. "My sides are badly in need of massaging after witnessing the spectacle." [3]

There was plenty going on backstage in Philadelphia too, thanks partly to Johnson's determination to hit on Waters while he was there. Though she admired him and enjoyed watching his sparring routine from the wings every night, Waters treated Johnson with what she calls "distant respect", thinking she'd have little in common with a star of that magnitude. Johnson himself had other ideas. One night, Waters was relaxing in her dressing room between shows in Philadelphia when he sent his valet round to suggest she come and talk to him. She replied that, if Johnson wanted a meeting, then why didn't he come round to her dressing room instead. "The valet got an odd look on his face," Waters writes. "I guess no colored person had ever responded like that before to an invitation from his boss. When Jack Johnson said 'Come' they all came running. Especially the girls."

A few minutes later, Johnson himself knocked at Waters' dressing room door and politely asked if he could come in. Waters let him to do so but turned down his invitation to dinner that night. This is her own description of the conversation that followed:

*"'But why not?' he asked. 'Why won't you have dinner with me?'*

*"I told him I wanted to make myself clear. 'That white girl I see hanging around the theater, Mr Jack – isn't she your wife?'*

*"'No, she's just a friend.'*

*"'But I never see you with any colored girls.'*

*"'I have nothing against colored girls,' he said. 'And I'd be proud to be seen out with you, Ethel.' But I wouldn't have dinner with him. And Jack Johnson was intrigued. I don't think he had met one other colored girl since becoming famous who didn't try to track him down."*

The two stayed friends all the way through to Johnson's death in 1946. "He regarded me as one of his buddies and, whenever we were in the same town, he'd come to see me," Waters writes. "Once in a while, he'd say, 'I could like a woman like you, Ethel.' But I'd only have to say 'Now, Jack,' and we'd laugh and go back to the more satisfactory buddy-pal basis."

As Waters dealt with Johnson at that first meeting, her bandmates were having some trouble of their own at the Philadelphia boarding house where they'd all been lodged. Here's Bushell again:

*"We stayed at the Horseshoe Hotel, where all the toughs lived. While we were there someone tried to rob me, but I pulled my gun and ran everybody out of the room. In those days, a Negro didn't have much protection from the law and so had to protect himself. [...] Charlie Jackson kept a .45 in his violin case and Buddy Aiken had a .25 automatic under his derby. When Buddy took off his hat, he meant business.* [4]

*"In Philadelphia I got full of that Prohibition gin and accidentally shot a girl who was trying to frame me. I was fooling around with two girls and one of them didn't know it was supposed to be on the QT, so she told the other and they both jumped on me about it. I was half-drunk, so I said 'Who do you think I am? I'll show you who I am!' I shot down at the floor, but the bullet glanced up and struck her in the heel. That quieted everyone down."* [5]

### Baltimore: Regent Theatre, Nov 28-30.

The *Baltimore Afro-American* of December 2, 1921, has

this review of the show:

> *"Preceding Miss Waters' appearance, her eight jazz boys treated the audience to as fine an exhibition of jazz playing as has ever been heard here, white or black. Every one of them is a master of his particular instrument, and Raymond Green at the drums was a veritable 'knockout'. His equal for comedy in this department has never come this way. [...] Miss Waters' voice is of mezzo quality with that mournful sweetness that is regarded as characteristic of the Southern Negro. She is a fine actress and knows just how much to put in and how much to leave out of her song interpretations in order to make them effective."*

Thanks to reviews like this one, we can start to imagine what the show was like to watch. Individual members of the band had concocted some little comedy skits of their own to enliven the opening stages if the evening, one of which was cooked up by Green and Bushell. "I was a cop and Green was a preacher," Bushell remembers. "He'd be standing there on the street preaching at what looked like an altar, but it would be his xylophone, covered up. I'd come out in a cop uniform and chase him off. Ray Green was a very funny character, and a good drummer too." Gus Aiken's "laughing cornet" routine quickly became another audience favourite.

Finally, the whole band would join together and blast through a short instrumental set while their singer waited offstage. When he sensed the crowd was ready to explode, Henderson gave Waters a big introduction and she'd stroll on, often producing an excited ovation before she'd even sung a note. Every night would climax with her singing *Down Home Blues* – still by far her biggest hit – and that was her pet Pekinese's cue to trot out of the dressing room to join his mistress on stage, pawing at her dress there to let her know he wanted to be picked up. The dog's name was Bubbles, and he'd been present at quite enough of Waters' shows to know that *Down Home Blues* meant the night was nearly over and it was his turn for some attention at last. Most nights, Waters would take her final bows with the tiny dog already cradled in her arms.

**Pittsburgh, early December.**
**Wheeling, WV, early December.**
It was in Pittsburgh that Lester Walton joined the tour as road manager and chief publicist. Born in 1882, he was a prominent Black journalist, related by marriage to Fred Moore, the publisher of *New York Age*, where Walton worked as the paper's theatre editor. He handled most of the practicalities of getting everyone in the right place at the right time, made sure the tour got plenty of news coverage at every stop and joined with Booker T Washington's Tuskegee Institute to arrange civil rights meetings in many of the Southern towns they visited. [6]

Walton was a little older and a great deal more responsible than most of the Troubadours, so he was also given charge of the tour's cash float, which he kept in a suitcase that never left his side. Each night, he'd collect their share of the show's box office money in used notes, stuff them into his suitcase and prepare to move on to the next stop. Whenever there was food or accommodation to be paid for, a cop to be bribed, or any one of the thousand other expenses needed to keep the show on the road, he'd reach for his case again. At a bare minimum, the Troubadours' party had a dozen mouths to feed – perhaps as many as 15 or 20 – so it's safe to assume that suitcase emptied out just as fast as it filled.

**Ohio: 11 stops, December.**
This leg included shows in Steubenville, Youngstown,

Zanesville, Cleveland, Akron, Mansfield, Marion, Columbus, Springfield, Dayton and Middletown. They'd return to Ohio for a Cincinnati gig in February 1922.

**Meanwhile, back in New York.**
As the tour moved through Ohio, Pace was busy cooking up a new publicity stunt. Towards the end of December, he issued a press release announcing Waters had signed a brand-new contract with Black Swan undertaking not to marry at any time in the coming year. She'd received so many marriage proposals in the past few months, he gravely explained, that the label was worried she might abandon the tour to wed a rich suitor instead. Why, as recently as the gig in West Virginia, a handsome young doctor had almost succeeded in tempting her away! The new contract, he added, would lock Waters in, not just with the anti-marriage clause itself, but also by making her "the highest-salaried colored phonograph star in this country".

Publicity stunt or not, this was far too good a story to ignore. The newspapers fell on it with glee. "Ethel must not marry," the *Chicago Defender* breathlessly declared in its December 24 headline. Ethel's new fee for every Black Swan show she played and every Black Swan disc she cut was a sum "that most people would be glad to earn in a month".

The part about the increased pay was probably true – it made sense for Pace to bind Waters with the strongest golden handcuffs he could find at this point - but reporters must have realised the stuff about marriage proposals was nonsense. Waters' relationship with Williams was an open secret throughout the entertainment industry and would not have come as news to anyone who'd witnessed the two women's antics in Harlem either. They'd flirt together on stage whenever the Troubadours show gave them a chance, so some sharper members of the audience may well have caught on too. Even in the 1920s, people tended to give showbiz folk a little extra latitude in sexual matters, so few thought it was anything to make a fuss about.

It would have taken a superhuman effort for Pace to remain unaware of Waters' sexual preferences. Perhaps he was privately rather shocked by how she behaved, but if so, he had the good sense to keep those views to himself. Why risk upsetting his biggest star over something as trivial as her choice of bedmate? Waters herself took the press release in her stride and happily signed the new contract, knowing it would boost her pay, help sell extra tour tickets and perhaps even act to discourage those few pestering males who still hadn't got the message.

The guys in the band often picked up admirers of their own, and never hesitated to call on Waters when the time came to disentangle themselves next morning. Her matey, bantering relationship with Bushell, Aiken and the rest meant she was always glad to oblige. "No matter which musician it was, he'd tell the unwanted girl that I was his girlfriend," she writes. "He'd even get me to bawl him out in front of her. The spurned girls talked together, and word got around that I was sleeping with the whole outfit. But they had not that kind of interest in me, nor I in them."

### Louisville, KY: Lincoln Theatre, Dec 25-31.

The Jazz Masters were relaxing after one of the Lincoln Theatre shows when a local madame called Tiny Tally came backstage and announced she was throwing a party for them. Tally, as they soon discovered, owned seven "buffet flats" in Louisville – brothels to you and me – and counted many of the city's richest and most powerful men among her customers. "The mayor, the chief of police and everybody else were her clients," Bushell writes. "Tiny was about forty years old and she had so much money she didn't know what to do with it." [7, 8]

Bushell's ideally placed to tell this story, because it was him Tally took a fancy to. Each morning during the band's Louisville stay, she'd stuff $500 into his pocket, and send him off to enjoy a day at the track. He'd spend a little of it, stash the rest, and then tell Tally he'd lost the lot. Next day, she'd give him another $500 and send him off to the track again. If Bushell would just agree to stay on in Louisville, she said, he'd never have to work another day in his life. "She loved the ground I walked on," Bushell writes. "Every night was a party. She'd bring her various hookers in, but I know she threatened them. 'Don't you bother with that one. That little young one over there, that's mine'." [9]

There was a bit of a fracas at Tally's place one night when her old boyfriend turned up and objected to the news that he'd been replaced, but she soon dealt with that. The real trouble came on the last night of the Louisville run, when Bushell told her he'd be moving on to St Louis with the rest of the band straight after the show. By then, he had $2,000 stashed away from his trips to the races – enough to make any young man feel like a millionaire in those days. Here's his own account again:

*"As I was getting ready to leave the theater, there she was: she had backed her Packard right up to the stage door, and she was sitting at the exit with a razor in her hand. 'Bouchard,' she said, waving her razor at me. 'You're going to stay with me.' The Packard's door opened, and I walked in, and we went back to her house.* [10]

*"At about five or six in the morning – it was daylight by now – she went out in the kitchen to fix some ham and eggs. [...] When she went out, I picked up my clarinet and my bag and went out the side door. I ran about fifteen blocks to the railway station, right down the middle of the street. If the cops had been there, they'd have shot me.*

*"When I got there, I went directly into the men's*

*room and I gave the porter a five-dollar tip. I told him,
'If you see Tiny Tally, you didn't see me. You come
back and tell me when my train for Chicago comes in.
Sure enough, he came in later and said she'd been
there looking for me, but that she was gone now, and I
could board my train for Chicago."* [11, 12]

## St Louis: Booker Washington Theatre, Jan 1-7, 1922.
## Indianapolis: Washington Theatre, Jan 9-15.

With his clarinet player still missing in action, Henderson
was forced to find a replacement wherever he could.
Sometimes the venue's house orchestra was able to lend
him someone, who'd then have to learn the Jazz Masters'
set in record time. Even with one of these stand-ins playing,
the band continued to get rave reviews. "Congratulations
on your wonderful show which opened here today to record
business," the St Louis theatre's manager cabled to Pace.
"Predict increase in sales of your product by thousand per
cent."

## Meanwhile, back in New York.

On January 14, 1922, a Columbia ad appeared in *New York
Age* listing the singer Carroll Clark as one of nine
"exclusive colored artists" whose work was "produced
exclusively on Columbia Records". Pace, who'd signed
Clark to an exclusive Black Swan deal several months
earlier, was incensed. Not only was the ad an outright lie,
but he knew that Clark had quit Columbia for Black Swan
precisely because the white-owned label had treated him so
badly.

Clark had recorded a few ballads for Columbia
before Pace even approached him, but these died on the
vine through lack of any worthwhile promotion. Columbia
refused even to put his photograph on these records'
sleeves, insisting Black faces must be linked only to "the
type of song that has come to be associated in the popular

95

mind with the sophisticated 'coon'." That's when he walked out and signed a deal with Black Swan instead.

Pace's attitude was very different. He'd immediately given Clark Angelo Mascheroni's *For All Eternity* to record as one of Black Swan's three debut discs and distributed thousands of pictures of the singer to publicise Black Swan's coup in signing him. It was only after this boost to Carroll's profile that Columbia had decided to re-release their old sides of his and flag them up in ads.

Clark's third disc for Black Swan – this one pairing *Swing Low Sweet Chariot* with *One Sweetly Solemn Thought* – had been released just two weeks before the Columbia ad appeared. "Mr Pace is advised by his attorneys that Columbia's campaign is calculated to damage the sale of the Black Swan record," the *Chicago Defender* reported. "A suit for damages is being prepared accordingly." The same story mentions complaints that another white-owned label had been bribing Pace's dealers to scratch Black Swan records before selling them on to customers. The idea was to persuade people these discs were badly made, and so sabotage the label's sales. [13, 14]

## Chicago: Grand Theatre, Jan 16-29.

Bushell made it to Chicago and met with Gus Aiken at a restaurant there – but his troubles weren't over yet. "As we were leaving, these three big white fellows crossed the street towards us," he writes. "I pulled my gun and Gus took out his knife. They said, 'Leave it right there! Drop it!' I never saw so many guns in my life. They were detectives."

The three cops cuffed Bushell and Aiken, then locked them in a cell at Clark Street police station. The weather in Chicago that night was so cold, Bushell says, that the nickel handcuffs froze to their wrists, leaving a visible mark there for years to come. "They never booked us, but they kept us in jail for three days," he writes. "It turned out a lot of cops had been killed in New York that year, and when they found out we were from New York, they held us. Buddy Aiken and Charlie Jackson, our violinist, finally found us and we were bailed out. It took all the money I had to pay [the bondsman] and the lawyer. But all this trouble saved me from Tiny Tally! She had come to Chicago looking to kill me. She finally left after two days, while I was still in jail."

That's how Henderson found himself missing not only his clarinetist, but also his cornet player as the first of the Chicago gigs came around. Once again, it was the venue's house orchestra that came to his rescue, lending him both Buster Bailey and Raymond Woodson to fill the empty chairs. [15]

Demand for tickets in Chicago was so high that the band's initial one-week stint at the Grand was extended to two. This gave the Troubadours a chance to collect themselves for a few days rather than being constantly on the move. Waters, who'd long yearned to hear a bit of grit in Henderson's piano playing, took this opportunity to sit him down with a set of piano rolls by the great boogie-woogie player Jimmy Johnson. These rolls contained a series of perforations like those on an old-fashioned computer punchcard, positioned in this case to "record" Johnson's playing as the roll was made. When loaded into a player piano, they'd instruct the instrument exactly what to do, reproducing Johnson's original rendition as the keys moved magically up and down.

Waters had huge respect for Henderson as an arranger and a bandleader, but constantly complained that his piano playing was too stuffy to capture the raw energy of proper blues and jazz. "Fletcher wouldn't give me what I call the 'damn-it-to-hell' bass," she writes. "That chump-chump-chump stuff that real jazz needs. All through the tour I kept nagging at him. I said he couldn't play as I wanted him too."

Presented with the Johnson piano rolls in Chicago, Henderson became obsessed with proving her wrong. "Fletch began to practice," Waters writes. "He got so perfect listening to James Johnson play on the player piano that he could press down the keys as the roll played, never missing a note. Naturally, he began to be identified with that kind of music, which isn't his kind at all." It was this tuition which paved the way for all Henderson's later success in jazz. Without Waters' determined nagging, it's a path he may never have discovered. [16]

Pace came up with another publicity stunt while the show was in Chicago, this one a dinner party hosted by Alberta Hunter at her home there. Hunter's first record for Black Swan, pairing *Bring Back the Joys* with *How Long, Sweet Daddy, How Long?* had been a big hit for the company, making her the closest thing Waters had to a rival there. Pace persuaded Hunter to have Waters, Williams and a few other guests over to her house one night, knowing this would guarantee the show a few paragraphs in the gossip pages just as it was about to embark on its Southern leg.

The only snag in this plan was that Hunter couldn't cook, so the job of preparing the meal fell to her girlfriend Carrie Mae Ward – though there's no mention of her being a guest at the party itself. Accounts of the evening suggest that Waters and Williams were in a rowdy mood, and that Hunter did not always appreciate the salty language they used at the table. She'd already begun to resent the fact that Black Swan never spent as much on promoting her records as they did on Waters', and seeing Williams queening it up at the table while her own partner sweated away in the kitchen can't have done much to improve her mood. She hid it well, though. "All voted Miss Hunter a charming hostess," the *Chicago Defender* declared. [17]

**Meanwhile, back in New York.**
On January 20, 1922, Harlem's Manhattan Casino staged a national blues singing competition before a large and highly-respectable audience. One of the people attending was Caruso's widow – a mark of just how accepted this music was now becoming in polite white society. The contest was decided by audience applause, and victory went to a newcomer called Trixie Smith, singing her own song *Trixie's Blues*. Pace signed her a few days later and released the song in February. Soon, she'd be another of the label's most valuable stars. [18]

**Gary, IN: Orpheum Theatre, Jan 30-Feb 1.**
**Cincinnati: Emery Hall, Feb 2-4.**
These were the tour's final two gigs before it moved on to Memphis and over 30 other towns and cities throughout the Jim Crow south.

## Half the band quits

*"We find during the first eleven months of this year a reign of barbarism that would put to shame the savages of the dark ages. Fifty-two lynchings, more than one a week, have been staged in the 'land of the free and the home of the brave' in the past eleven months, 48 of this number, including one woman, being members of our group. Mississippi leads with 13, Georgia being second with 10; South Carolina and Louisiana tie for third place with five each."*

**- *Chicago Defender* editorial, December 3, 1921.**

Let's rewind now to the final nights of the Troubadours' Grand Theatre run in Chicago, and to the band meeting that Henderson and Waters called there. With the tour's lengthy Southern run just about to begin, it was time to acknowledge the dangers everyone knew this would present, and to let each individual make their own decision about what to do next. For an all-Black troupe of players in the America of 1922, touring the South meant being insulted and demeaned at every turn, and forced to endure conditions even more basic than those they'd had to put up with on the rest of the TOBA circuit. But it didn't stop there.

·     NAACP figures showed white mobs had lynched 65 people in 1920 and another 52 in the first 11 months of 1921. Almost all the victims were Black and almost all had died in the very states the Troubadours were about to visit. The "crimes" being punished by these brutally sadistic murders could be as trivial as failing to step out of a white man's path quickly enough or daring to glance at his daughter as she passed in the street. In many of the towns the Troubadours were scheduled to play, any group of Black strangers from New York was going to stand out – particularly if they had a little money in their pockets – and that could spark the kind of resentment that soon turned ugly. As the band surveyed their planned route through Mississippi, Georgia and Texas, they had good reason to be nervous. [1]

Waters herself was adamant that the risk had to be faced. The jazz and blues music they'd all built their careers on was created in the Southern states, she reminded the assembled musicians. It was only right that the Black people living there got a chance to hear it played as only the Jazz Masters could. Half the eight-strong band agreed with her, but the other half did not: Bushell, Jackson and the two Aiken brothers gave notice they'd be quitting before the tour set off for Memphis. This meant giving up four very good jobs with no clear idea what they were going to do to replace the lost income, but still their own decision was clear. "In those days, you went South at the risk of your life," Bushell writes. "So many incidents occurred; you weren't even treated as a human being."

Henderson and Waters immediately set about finding replacements, calling in whatever favours they could in Pittsburgh, St Louis and Chicago. By the time the first of the Southern gigs came round, they'd installed Joe Smith, George Brashear and Clarence Robinson on cornet, trombone and clarinet respectively. Presumably, they found a new violinist to replace Jackson too, but if so that name seems to have vanished from the record.

The four departing band members had just enough money between them to get to Pittsburgh, where Earl Hines had a residency at Duquesne Gardens. He let them play a "pass-the-hat" set there before his own band went on, which raised the price of four train tickets to New York. A spot more busking on the train secured a meal on board, then they were finally back home. Bushell, so recently a wealthy man, had to borrow 25 cents from a Penn Station porter to call his father for a lift home.

# Four months of Jim Crow

*"We were playing colored theaters, but the white people wanted to see me and hear my songs. When your act went over good in these showhouses you gave two performances at midnight for exclusively white audiences. [...] We had to do two of the extra shows in every town we visited on that trip. We found ourselves applauded by the Ofays in the theater and insulted by them on the streets."*

**- Ethel Waters, *His Eye is On the Sparrow*.**

**Memphis: Palace Theatre, Feb 13-19, 1922.**

Southern leg of the tour begins. They wouldn't return north till the middle of June.

**Arkansas: Four stops, February 20-28.**

Shows at Miller's Theatre in Pine Buff, The Mosaic Temple Theatre in Little Rock, Hot Springs Auditorium and an unidentified theatre in Fort Smith.

Waters' records had gained her a lot of white fans by this stage of the tour, and the TOBA theatre owner in Little Rock wasn't daft enough to turn this extra ticket revenue away. There wasn't quite enough demand among the town's white folk to organise a full extra show just for them, but he did agree to set a section of the Mosaic Temple's auditorium aside for white patrons only. When Waters stepped out on stage that night, she was delighted to see he'd positioned this section right at the back of the hall, just as white owners always did with their own crows' nest seating. "They weren't the best down-front seats," she chuckles in her book. "Those were kept for the colored patrons. For once, the dominant race found itself segregated and in the rear."

At another small town in the South, the Black theatre's white owner agreed to admit both races into his divided auditorium but insisted that even the collection of tickets at the door must be rigorously segregated. Walton would have to help out by collecting the Black patrons' tickets, while the owner himself would collect the white ones. In the event, the eager crowd rushed in so fast that both me were forced to simply grab whichever ticket someone thrust at them first.

## Oklahoma: Two stops, March 1-4.

Shows in Muskogee and at Ardmore Convention Hall.

Press ads ahead of the Ardmore show called Waters "the greatest and highest-salaried colored phonograph star in the land". With her on the night would be "her big aggregation of colored syncopators, singers and comedians" who'd "gained fame throughout the United States" as "the cleanest and snappiest colored attraction on tour". [1]

## Texas: Eight stops, March 13 – April 15.

Shows in Paris, Fort Worth, Waco, Dallas (at the Pythian Temple), Austin (Lyric Theatre), Galveston, Tyler and Houston Auditorium.

The Troubadours were apprehensive about their Paris gig. February's Black newspapers had been full of stories about a particularly nasty lynching in nearby Texarkana and the week of white vigilante violence that followed. Not only that, but the previous July, a Black orchestra leader called Gordon Harrison had been kidnapped from a show in Paris itself by four masked men, who drove him two miles from town, whipped him and then let him go. This, they told him, was "a warning to all negroes to be careful in their relations with white people". It was incidents like this which led a Bowie County judge to say in February 1922 that the area was showing "more lawlessness and a worse kind of lawlessness" than he'd seen at any time in the past 50 years. [2, 3, 4]

In the event, the Black Swan troupe was pleasantly surprised by the courteous reception they got in Paris, playing a ballroom date where Black and white couples were allowed to mix freely on the dancefloor. They moved on to Fort Worth with a sigh of relief, but the stress of touring in a region where people like them could be so casually beaten or murdered at any moment never let up. As Waters herself says in the quote topping this chapter, many white ticket-buyers saw no contradiction in cheering the Troubadours' performance to the rafters while they were on stage, then spitting the vilest racial insults at them in the street next morning

By April 1, the show had reached Houston, which turned out to be a very bad bit of timing. Walton's suitcase was almost empty at the time, and they'd hoped to find a few impromptu gigs to top it up before their show at the city's Auditorium in two weeks' time. What they'd forgotten was that this was Lent, and that Houston's religious principles meant all its showbiz venues would be closed until Easter Sunday arrived on April 16. That was a pretty lean fortnight for everyone involved, but nothing new for most of the band. At last, the Auditorium gig came round, allowing Walton to clear the debts they'd run up in Houston and pay everyone's rail fare on to New Orleans. [5]

"We were stranded everywhere on that trip," Waters writes, explaining that one reason was the rivalry between various Black fraternal organisations. "They were jealous of one another and would knife and boycott any attraction not booked through their lodge," she writes. "Everywhere we went, we were told we were wonderful but had made the ghastly error of booking through the wrong organisation. If we worked through the local colored Elks, we were informed that next time we should contact the Knights of Pythias. If we were doing business with the Knights of Pythias in the next town, it should have been the Elks. It was as though they said: 'Next time, instead of contacting the sons of bitches, work with us, the bitches of sons'."

**Meanwhile, back in New York.**

As the tour progressed, Black Swan's record sales were still going from strength to strength. On March 21, 1922, Pace wrote to DuBois telling him he'd just signed a deal with a big Philadelphia distributor who'd agreed to take 3,000 of the label's discs every month for the next year. "Within a short time we hope to close several other such contracts, which will bring our production up to two or three times the size it was last year," he wrote. This fits broadly with the production figures Pace gives elsewhere: 2,500 records made each day at the end of 1921, against 6,000 or so a year later.

If he was going to satisfy this demand, Pace knew he could no longer rely on the Wisconsin plant alone. He had some irons in the fire there too – but that's a story which will have to wait a while.

**New Orleans: Lyric Theatre, April 17-23.**

The Troubadours had a solid week of gigs booked at the Lyric and broke the house records there with ease. Waters and the band proved so popular that the *New Orleans Daily Item*, one of the biggest white newspapers in the whole of the South, arranged a special Friday night radio appearance for them on its partner station WGV.

This historic broadcast would make Waters the first Black woman ever to sing live on US radio, and WGV marked the occasion by waiving its normal rules against Black visitors entering the studio by its front door. Well, waived them for some of the troupe, anyway: Waters and Walton, who'd been involved in organising the broadcast, were ushered in through the main entrance when they arrived, but Henderson and the rest of the band told to trudge round to the tradesmen's entrance at the rear of the building. Suddenly, it was Mr high-and-mighty Henderson watching low-down Tenth Avenue get all the perks, and you could forgive Waters a small smile at that.

WGV's transmitter was powerful enough to ensure the band's performance of *Down Home Blues* and a handful of their other live favourites was heard in five different states and parts of Mexico, giving Waters a radio audience of thousands. The *Savannah Tribune* was just one rival newspaper which recognised the broadcast's importance by making it front page news. New Orleans' Astoria Hotel rounded off the night with a thronged reception for the whole Troubadours company, where they were greeted as guests of honour. The two Ethels pulled out their most elegant gowns for the occasion and were rewarded with compliments for their style in *New York Age*. [6]

For a more raucous kind of fun in New Orleans, there was always the Lyric's midnight rambles. These were special late-night shows for the white audience, starting an hour or so after the evening's main show was done, and running through till the small hours. Shows like these – also known as midnight frolics – became very fashionable among white jazz and blues fans, who hoped to find something a little wilder there than they could get at their usual mainstream entertainments. ["The rambles] were different, a little nasty," the 1920s trumpeter Punch Miller told one interviewer. "They started at 11, ended around 2:00am." [7]

It was also in New Orleans that Henderson first stumbled across a young musician who'd have a huge influence on his future career. Killing time between shows one evening, he stopped by at the Elite, a tiny dancehall just two doors away from the Lyric, where he was struck by the talent and originality of the resident band's trumpeter. Cornering the lad between sets, he offered him a job playing with the Jazz Masters for the rest of their tour, followed by a spot in Black Swan's studio orchestra when they got back to New York. "I decided that youthful trumpeter would be great in our act," Henderson later told *Downbeat* magazine. "I asked him his name and found out it was Louis Armstrong."

Armstrong was just 20 at the time and had barely even begun his own musical career. For a complete unknown like him, let alone such a young one, the chance to join a respected and nationally-famous band was a huge opportunity. But still, he wavered. He told Henderson he'd have to consult his best friend, a lad called Zutty Singleton, who played drums in the Elite band Henderson had just been watching – but who had failed to impress him in anything like the same way. He told Armstrong to come round to the Lyric after tomorrow night's Troubadours show and give him his answer then.

"Louis told me he'd have to speak to his drummer,

because he couldn't possibly leave without him," Henderson says. "The next day, he was backstage at the theater to tell me that, much as he would love to go with us, he would have to be excused because the drummer wouldn't leave New Orleans." Some see this as a sign of admirable loyalty on the young Armstrong's part. Others think he simply lost his nerve and seized on Singleton as an excuse to stay put. [8]

Either way, it was a missed opportunity. "Had Louis joined Henderson's band at this point his career might have taken off faster than it did," Armstrong's biographer Laurence Bergreen writes. "Instead of rambling round Chicago and recording for little one-horse outfits like Gennett, he would have gone straight to New York and the centre of the Harlem Renaissance. He would have recorded for Black Swan and his star would have risen along with Fletcher Henderson's." [9]

## Alabama: Two stops, April 24-30, 1922.

Shows in Bessemer and Birmingham.

One of Waters' favourite stage effects during her part of the show relied on a dress she'd found which was infused with radium. In the 1920s, this material was thought to be a miraculous life-giving substance, used to add pizzazz and extra sales performance to everything from toothpaste and foodstuffs to cosmetics, suppositories and impotence treatments. Waters had no more idea of the dangers of radioactivity than anyone else did at the time, and she'd bought the radium dress simply because she knew it would glow in the dark. Each night on stage, when she came to a song called *If Ever You're Lonesome Just Telephone Me*, she'd signal with her fan to a theatre electrician in the wings, and he'd plunge the stage and auditorium into complete darkness. Right through this number, the only light anyone could see came from her frock's unearthly glow, casting its spectral illumination up at her face as she sang. [10]

The effect of this in 1922, particularly for an audience outside the big cities, must have been spectacular – but at the opening night in Bessemer it all went wrong. "That night he left two lights burning, spoiling the whole effect," Waters writes. "I sure pitched a bitch with that electrician. When he said it was the manager who messed up the lights-out cue, I jumped on that man too. I explained how important the dress that shone in the dark was to my number. 'Your people have never seen anything like it,' I told him in my rage."

There were more problems in Birmingham, although these came on the run's last night rather than its first. Some of the guys from the band, including George Brashear, took themselves off to the city's famous Tuxedo Junction neighbourhood after the final Birmingham show to have a little fun before they moved on to Nashville next day. This section of town at the intersection of Ensley Avenue and 19th Street was packed with bars and clubs, making it the centre of Black nightlife for miles around. It was Saturday night, so all the joints there would have have busy, packed to the seams with partying dancers.

Next morning, Lester Walton – who'd given the Tuxedo Junction trip a miss – was  enjoying what he'd hoped would be a quiet breakfast when Brashear burst in and told him two or three of the other band members had been arrested. A white cop had taken exception to the sight of Black New Yorkers enjoying themselves in his town and come up with some excuse to lock them up. Only Brashear had managed to slip away, watching from nearby as his friends were dragged off for a night in the cells. They'd still be there now, he told Walton.

Abandoning his breakfast, Walton headed off with

Brashear to the police station to see if he could get them freed. He explained to the desk sergeant that they had another important gig to get to next day, and that this lay 200 miles away in Nashville. So many people would be disappointed if it had to be cancelled. Could nothing be done to release his friends this morning on the understanding that they'd immediately leave town? The desk sergeant replied that, sadly, this being a Sunday, there was no court open to hear a plea for bail and so nothing could be done till Monday. Although…

Walton knew well what was coming next. If they'd care to post a $100 "bond" against the likely fines, the sergeant continued, then perhaps he could he see his way clear to letting their friends go. Oh, and perhaps Brashear had better leave his watch there as security too. Walton and Brashear were under no illusions they'd ever see either the money or the watch again – this was a bribe, pure and simple – but what choice did they have? The alternative was to scupper the Nashville gig, and perhaps those scheduled to follow in Chattanooga and Atlanta too. Walton produced the $100 from his trusty suitcase, Brashear unclasped his watch, and they collected their colleagues from the cell. If this was Alabama, then roll on Tennessee.

**Bijou Theatre, Nashville, May 1-7.**

**Liberty Theatre, Chattanooga, May 8.**

There were more changes in the support acts as the tour reached Nashville. Gulfport & Brown dropped out of the comedy bill and Williams found a new dance partner called Roscoe Wickham.

**Georgia: Five stops, May 9-16.**

Shows at Atlanta Auditorium, The Douglass Theatre in Macon, the Lenox Theatre in Augusta and Savannah's Municipal Auditorium.

The Troubadours pulled a disappointing crowd of only about 300 people at Savannah's Municipal Auditorium but did far better the following night at the city's Lincoln Theatre, where they added another midnight frolic to the main show. Waters' billing now called her "Queen of the Blues" – perhaps a conscious echo of Bessie Smith's billing as "Empress of the Blues".

### South Carolina: Two stops, May 18-19.

Shows in Columbia and at Greenville's Liberty Theatre.

### North Carolina: Four stops, May 23-30.

Shows at Charlotte Auditorium, Wilmington Academy of Music, Greensboro Grand Theatre and Raleigh Academy of Music.

All three of these shows set aside a small section of the auditorium to seat white patrons only. In the case of Wilmington, this comprised 100 seats, which were sold through a cigar store in the town rather than any of the outlets open to Black buyers. Anyone going along would see "the greatest negro show touring the country," the *Wilmington Morning Star* promised its readers. The *Wilmington Tribune's* review was equally enthusiastic. "The crowd was left wide-eyed and gasping with astonishment for the company has class written all over it," the paper's critic gushed. "Ethel Waters is headlined, but was forced to share her honors with Ethel Williams, a dancer of more ability than two-thirds of those who have ever played Wilmington. Her act sent the crowd into paroxysms of the wildest delight." [11, 12]

The white folks' seating at Greensboro comprised the right-hand stalls at $1.00 and the lower boxes on that side at $1.25. The rest of the hall was given over to Black patrons, who paid $1.00 for seats in the left and centre stalls or the first six rows of the balcony. The rest of the main balcony went at 75 cents, while the second balcony was priced at just 50 cents. It's pretty clear from this split that Greensboro expected no more than about 20% of the total audience to be white. In Raleigh, though, they set aside the whole of the ground-floor stalls for whites, consigning Black patrons to the balcony above. [13]

**Virginia: Two stops, June 5-8.**

Shows at the Rayo Theatre in Richmond and Attuck's Theatre in Norfolk. The Richmond show pulled in one of the biggest crowds of the whole tour, with over 4,000 people a night attending.

**Baltimore: Douglass Theatre, June 11-17.**

The tour returns to the relative safety and comfort of the north.

**Washington DC: Howard Theatre, late June.**

**Philadelphia: Standard Theatre, June 26-July 2.**

**New York: Lafayette Theatre, July 10-16.**

This return visit to Philadelphia is another of the few Troubadours shows where we have details of the full bill.

The evening started with Raymond Green's featured xylophone spot, followed by Sandy Burns performing a short farce called *Trouble in the House* with Sam Russell's theatre company. Then came The Three Zangarelles, an aerialist duo called Wells & Wells, Smith DeForest &

Smith and comedians Anderson & Gay. Williams and Wickham came next with their shimmy and shiver dance routines, then finally it was time for Waters and the Jazz Masters. The whole show ran for about two hours from start to finish.

The Lafayette in Harlem was the tour's final stop after eight months on the road. The Troubadours had played well over 50 towns in a total of 19 different states (and one Federal District). Anyone living east of a line between El Paso and Duluth could have found a gig in either their own or a neighbouring state. [14]

# Passing for coloured

*"Some white companies whose sales have been
affected by the sales of our records are using a
few short-sighted colored people in establishing
a Jim Crow annex to their business. They hope
to rid themselves of our competition in that way
and to reduce the Negro singer and musician to
the same status he had before we entered the
field."*

**- Black Swan ad in *Crisis*, January 1922.**

As we've seen, the combined effect of *Down Home Blues'*
success and the extra Black Swan discs sold everywhere
the Troubadours touched down gave the company's
finances a spectacular turnaround. An April 1922 report in
the *Chicago Defender* credits Black Swan with sales of
$100,658.21 over the six months to December 1, 1921, and
profits of $41,763.27 over the same period. Pace told *New
York Age* that his label had sold 400,000 records in the full
12 months. [1]

When DuBois saw his shareholder copy of the
accounts, he wrote to Pace saying they showed the
company in "a very satisfactory condition" and
congratulating him on "a fine year's work". Black Swan
was still only a tenth the size of giant labels like Victor but
ending its first year in profit was no small achievement –

particularly when, as the *Dallas Express* reminded its readers, every step along the way had been met with "underhand, malicious and persistent opposition of several of the large white companies". [2, 3]

White listeners were far more supportive, particularly the showbiz royalty who now saw Black Swan records as the must-have music at their parties. In July 1922, Marilyn Miller, the star of a Broadway musical called *Sally*, married Jack Pickford, Mary Pickford's brother and a movie star in his own right. Miller used this occasion to give her new husband a selection of Black Swan discs. "Miss Miller first heard these records through another member of the *Sally* cast and was so pleased with them that she sent several to her fiancé," the *Black Dispatch* reported. "After the wedding the records were placed on the machine and the whole party danced to the strains of Henderson's Dance Orchestra and made merry as Ethel Waters sang *Oh Daddy, Jazzin' Babies Blues* and *That Da Da Strain*. It is now becoming quite a fad with many stars of the theatrical profession, who have found something different in these all-colored records, to have them sent to their friends in various parts of the country." [4]

At last, Pace felt, he could look to the future with a little confidence. The manufacturing facilities he rented in Wisconsin were already struggling to press enough records to satisfy the new orders Black Swan had pouring in, so that's where he turned his attention first. The Wisconsin plant's owners – who also owned Paramount records, remember – had been happy enough to let Pace press discs there when Black Swan was too small to worry about, but he knew he'd face nothing but obstruction from them now. Black Swan's growth meant it was starting to appear on Paramount's radar just as Paramount itself was planning to launch a race label. How long would it be till someone there realised Black Swan was entirely dependent on the

Wisconsin plant, and used Paramount's influence there to torpedo Pace's manufacturing?

What Black Swan needed was a pressing plant of its own so, in March 1922, Pace joined with a white record executive called John Fletcher to buy the bankrupt Remington Phonograph Company's plant in Long Island City. This was the same plant he'd attempted to buy a year earlier but been blocked from doing so by the white-owned labels. It was their scuppering of Pace's first bid that had driven him out to Wisconsin in the first place. Now he had his revenge. Mixed-race partnerships like the one he'd sealed with Fletcher were very unusual in the recording industry at this time – perhaps ever unprecedented – but both men were ready to break the taboo if that's what it took to get the deal done.

John Fletcher had started his musical career as a cornet player, then got interested in recording technology and set up his own label in 1914. It was called Operaphone and specialised in white dance bands and light opera. The company's major asset was a two-storey concrete building on Long Island City's Meadow Street, which contained all the machinery Operaphone needed to manufacture its own discs. The label went bust in early 1921, which is when Pace made his first attempt to buy its plant.

On that occasion, it went to Remington instead, in a deal which transferred all Operaphone's assets to a new label called Olympic, releasing white dance bands' records and the Hawaiian slack-string guitar discs then in vogue. Remington held the controlling interest in Olympic but allowed Fletcher to stay on as the new label's company secretary. A year later, Remington went bust too, taking Olympic down with it, and that left the plant and all its machinery to be auctioned off at fire sale prices.

The March 1922 auction catalogue lists the assets on sale as: "a fully-equipped plant for the manufacture of phonograph records, phonograph records completed and in the course of completion, all materials and property used in the manufacture of phonograph records, all patents, copyrights and trademarks, all office and factory furniture and fixtures, together with the complete equipment of the Olympic Disc Record Corporation". This was everything Pace needed, tied up in a single package. Most crucially of all, the plant was 700 miles closer to Black Swan's Manhattan offices and recording studios than the Wisconsin plant was.

Pace and Fletcher bought everything listed as a job lot and set up a new company called The Fletcher Record Company to operate the plant for Black Swan's exclusive use. Fletcher was installed as president of the new firm and Pace as its vice-president and treasurer. Fletcher ran the place day-to-day while Pace returned to wider Black Swan business. "The management of the plant will continue in the hands of the present skilled white employees," *New York Age* told its readers. "But as soon as colored men can be trained to take their places, they will be employed." (5)

\*\*\*

As Pace finalised the Long Island City deal, competition from the white-owned labels was growing fiercer than ever. The lucrative new market Okeh and Black Swan had uncovered was now producing sales of over $100,000 a month from African-American consumers alone, and everyone wanted to grab a piece. (6)

Like any small label, Black Swan could create stars, but often found it very difficult to keep them. Pace had given Alberta Hunter her first record deal, releasing her debut disc before even *Down Home Blues* came out. *Bring Back the Joys* sold well for Black Swan, but Pace was able to get only two more sides out of her before Paramount poached her. Hunter's *Don't Pan Me*, recorded in July 1922, was the disc Paramount used to launch its whole race imprint, and Pace knew she'd never be priced within his range again.

Columbia and Paramount were the first of the majors to get their race labels up and running, but Victor and the rest weren't far behind, and they were all keen to poach Black talent too. In the first six months of 1923 alone, Black Swan went from having half the nation's Black recording stars on its books to just one in five. Bessie Smith, Ma Rainey and Louis Armstrong all made their recording debuts in that year, and all for white-owned labels happy to encourage the kind of earthy material Pace tended to disdain. The Smith and Rainey debuts were big hits for Columbia and Paramount respectively, shifting over 100,000 copies each and underlining the fact that most Black record buyers still lived in the rural South, far from the Harlem Renaissance sophistication which Pace personified. Without the push Black Swan provided, the white majors may have taken another year or two to wake up to the pool of Black talent surrounding them, leaving God knows how many careers still-born, but that thought can't have been much consolation to Pace at the time. [7]

Often, the white-owned labels employed Black talent scouts like Paramount's Mayo Williams to put an acceptable face on their poaching expeditions, knowing that this would soften any suggestion of racial betrayal the proposed defection might carry. White executives could now see there was a lot of money to be made in signing up the best Black singers and dialled down their old contempt just enough to steer some of that money in their own direction. These changes were only skin-deep, though, as we can see from the way these same white companies continued to picture Black people in their ads: thick lips, bulging eyes and expressions of comic bemusement were still the norm. [8]

However much Pace tried to argue that the big white-owned labels would simply exploit Black artists, it was their fatter wallets that generally won the day. In every case, they were able to offer upfront payments, recording fees and promotional budgets which even the new Black Swan could not hope to match. Pace had been able to go toe-to-toe with Okeh when advertising in the Black press, because the ads they could afford were no bigger than his own. But once the big boys started pushing their own race label releases in the same papers, their massive ads drowned out Black Swan's promotion with ease. Meanwhile, the white companies' covert dirty tricks campaign against Pace was continuing, including – or so it seemed at the time – the planting of a bomb in the Long Island City plant's coal supply.

This happened on September 2, 1922, and produced a front-page story in the *Richmond Planet*:

*"Considerable excitement was caused Saturday in the manufacturing district of New York by the finding of a bomb in the coal delivered to the manufacturing plant of the Pace Phonograph Corporation, makers of Black Swan records, at Meadow and Creek streets in Long Island City. The bomb was of the shrapnel type, heavily loaded and capped, and capable of blowing up the entire plant.*

*"The fireman discovered the bomb after it was in his shovel and just as he was about to plunge it into the furnace. A moment later and there would have been an explosion that would have wrecked the boilers and damaged the plant, probably killing or injuring the 25 employees working there.*

*"Investigation was made by the bomb squads of the Police Department and the Fire Department. Just where the bomb came from could not be ascertained as the Pace Company uses nearly 30 tons of coal per month, deliveries from two coal companies are being made almost daily and each had just delivered several tons of coal.*

*"It is presumed the bomb was put into the coal by someone connected with the coal miners' strike. The officials of the company were alarmed at first lest it were the work of competitors who were seeking to destroy their business in Black Swan Records, the sale of which has so seriously interfered with other phonograph records made by the white companies."* [9]

The man who'd discovered the bomb was John Schmidt, one of the shovel team responsible for keeping the plant's boilers fed with coal. As all his workmates fled around him, he'd calmly picked up the bomb and carried it to the plant's admin offices, where someone called the police. It was found to be an old artillery shell from World War One, though now missing both its cap and its fuse. "Dr George W Koch, a chemical expert attached to the Fire Prevention Board in Brooklyn, made an examination of the missile and pronounced it a three-inch shrapnel shell with power enough to have blown up the building if it had gone off," said the *Dallas Express*. "The casing was rusted and it had lain concealed for a long time." [10]

Given everything else the white record companies had put him through, you can hardly blame Pace for initially assuming the bomb was their work too. He never mentions it again, though, not even in the long letters he'd later write to PPC shareholders listing every last obstacle Black Swan had been faced with along the way, and that does suggest he came to believe it was bad luck rather than malice that brought the shell to his own plant. Just like him, we'll never know for sure. [11]

\*\*\*

Pace decided the time had come for drastic action. His ads for Black Swan had always stressed the company's Black ownership and talent base, but now he upped the ante even further, with ads like the "Jim Crow annex" one topping this chapter. "Passing for Colored has become popular since we established Black Swan Records as the only genuine Colored Records, sung by Colored Artists and made by a Colored Company," another of Pace's December 1922 ads declared. "At least three white concerns are now catering to Negro buyers and advertising in Negro newspapers who never did so previously. One Company issues a catalogue and calls its Record 'the new Race Record'. In other words, it is attempting to 'Pass for Colored'. [...] Don't be deceived. We repeat: The Only Genuine Colored Record is Black Swan'." [12, 13]

He rammed this message home again and again. Black Swan had "the only records made and controlled exclusively by Negroes". It was a company where "all stockholders are Colored, all artists are Colored, all employees are Colored". His records were "the only records using exclusively Negro voices and Musicians", with "Every one made by Colored Singers". [14]

For Pace, Black Swan had always been an idealistic enterprise as much as a commercial one, and now he was hoping to persuade his artists and customers to take the same view. Unlike the white-owned labels, which simply wanted to extract money from Black people and place it in the pockets of white shareholders, Black Swan was pledged to keep its own profits in the community that generated them. Buy a Black Swan disc, Pace's new ads argued, and you could be sure your cash went to giving Black employees a job, helping Black artists to develop their work and enabling Black investors to continue pumping money back into their own neighbourhoods. If he'd had to boil his ads' message down to the more succinct form demanded today, it might have read: "Black Swan: All Black, all the time". [15]

As the new race imprints assailed Pace from every direction, each waving a chequebook far bigger than his own, taking a stand on Black Swan's idealism and integrity must have looked like his only chance to fight back. But this was a dangerous game, because Pace was doubling down on a promise he knew Black Swan had already broken.

*\*\*\**

Pace had broken his vow that all the label's talent was Black as early as 1921, when he began buying in the occasional side recorded by white musicians for another label and renaming the group involved to suggest they were Black. The first example was Black Swan 2025, released in November 1921, which paired two recent Olympic sides by Irving Weiss & his Ritz Carlton Orchestra but re-credited them to "Henderson's Novelty Orchestra".

Black Swan was still operating on a shoestring at that point, which limited Pace's ability to make new recordings, so buying in tracks from outside was sometimes his only option. The few Black bands then allowed to record hadn't had time to build up any back catalogue of their own, so it was the white musicians' sides or nothing. However queasy Pace may have felt about the deception, at least it allowed him to keep up a steady flow of Black Swan releases and, with luck, to boost the label's income too. On the odd occasions when a white band sold well for Black Swan, Pace was glad to pump the money back into the label's genuine Black talent.

No-one could have told from the music alone whether the Weiss/Henderson disc had been recorded by Black or white musicians, but in the context of the time that distinction did matter. Not only had Black Swan repeatedly made its "all-Black" pledge a key sales claim for the label, but some white artists did not take kindly to finding themselves reclassified as Black.

"The Original Dixieland Jazz Band had been an enormous success for the Victor record label in the 1917 to 1921 period," Mark Berresford told me in 2007. "They moved record companies in 1922 to record for Okeh who had a specific race records catalogue. The records by the Original Dixieland Jazz Band were issued in Okeh's general catalogue but were rumoured to be advertised as being by black artists. Nick La Rocca, who was the leader of the band, went berserk and cancelled the contract." [16]

Other white bands had the sense to treat race sales as simply a handy source of extra income. The Original Memphis Five, for example, recorded several sides for Gennett as "Ladd's Black Aces" and made no objection when a photograph of a Black band was used to advertise those discs in Gennett's race catalogue.

At first, Pace's white releases had been rare enough to be forgivable, but things began to get out of control in June 1922. US radio sales reached $60m in that year, beginning a steep climb which would take them to $358m just two years later. Record sales halved over roughly the same period and, as ever, it was small labels like Black Swan which suffered most. Faced with a depleted roster of artists, falling sales and all the costs of his recent expansion, Pace had only one option left. [17]

The Long Island City deal had brought with it John Fletcher's stash of masters from the defunct Olympic label: masters which had been recorded by white artists, but which Pace was now free to use at no extra cost. Telling himself it was only a temporary measure until the market improved, he sent Black Swan's renaming and reissue programme into overdrive. Often, the results were comical, as Yerkes Jazzarimba Orchestra became "Joe Brown's Alabama Band", Rudy Wiedoeft's Californians found themselves rechristened "Haynes Harlem Syncopators" and Margaret McKee was transformed into "Bessie Johnson". (18)

All this time, Pace continued to advertise Black Swan as releasing nothing but Black talent. One ad, placed in the *Chicago Defender* in July 1922, is headed with the words "DON'T BE DECEIVED! BLACK SWAN RECORDS Are the Only Exclusive Colored Records and Are Made by a Colored Company". Beneath this heading, it list ten new Black Swan discs, each one double-sided and hence making a total of 20 tracks in all. Of those 20 tracks, 14 are actually re-attributed white recordings from the old Olympic catalogue. "Mamie Jones", for example, is really Aileen Stanley, while "Ethel Waters' Jazz Masters" conceals both the Palace Trio on side A and the Van Eps Quartet overleaf.

Most of the tracks Pace recycled in this way had begun life on Fletcher's Olympic label, but he also bought in sides from Paramount, Puritan, LaBelle and Melody. On at least one occasion, he outsmarted himself, taking an Olympic recording by his old colleague Fletcher Henderson and needlessly reattributing that too. Henderson's Dance Players there found themselves renamed as "Sammy Swift's Jazz Band" for no reason at all.

No-one could have guessed Pace's deception from the discs' music alone, and it's unlikely anyone in the early

1920s had a big enough record collection to play the old Olympic sides and their Black Swan equivalents side-by-side. Most buyers, even if they'd known what was going on, probably wouldn't have cared. Pace's call for them to buy Black Swan discs for idealistic reasons had generally fallen on deaf ears, so why should they feel any sense of betrayal now? The real damage, I suspect, came when Black Swan's remaining artists realised what he was up to. Already tempted to desert the label for the greater cash rewards its white rivals could offer, they now had a perfect excuse to do so. If even Pace himself had dumped Black Swan's guiding principle, then it was clear they owed the label no particular loyalty either.

*Black Swan ad.* Chicago Defender, *July 15, 1922.*

# Pace battles Marcus Garvey

*"An unscrupulous demagogue who has
ceaselessly and assiduously sought to spread
among negroes distaste and hatred for all white
people."*
**- Pace on Garvey, February 1923.**

*"A business exploiter who endeavors to appeal
to the patriotism of the race by selling us
commodities at a higher rate than is charged in
the ordinary markets."*
**- Garvey on Pace, February 1923.**

In February 1923, Marcus Garvey, the Black separatist leader who headed the Universal Negro Improvement Association, was awaiting trial on year-old Federal charges of mail fraud. As the trial was about to begin, US Attorney General Harry Daugherty received an extraordinary letter.

Put together by eight prominent Black campaigners, journalists and entrepreneurs, this letter gave a damning assessment of Garvey's work and urged Daugherty to deport him at the first opportunity. "[It accuses Garvey] of a working alliance with the Ku Klux Klan," the *South Bend Tribune* told its readers. "The UNIA is characterized as an organization designed to foment hatred of whites by

Blacks, its members 'so fanatical they have threatened the death of their Negro opponents, actually assassinating in one instance'. The information on Garvey and his organization is expected by officials to prove invaluable in the government's probe." [1]

One of the men who signed that letter was Harry Pace. A few years earlier, he and Garvey had found a good deal to agree on, with both men championing the cause of racial uplift and feeling strongly that it must rest on the twin columns of both economic and cultural advancement. In early 1922, Garvey had even invited Pace to give a lecture at UNIA's Harlem headquarters. It was in how to achieve their ends that the two men so fundamentally differed: for Pace the work was all about gradually winning his people a just inclusion in every aspect of American society; for the more militant Garvey only complete separation of the races and a return to Africa would do.

Pace and the other successful African-Americans who signed the letter saw Garvey as a dangerous radical, whose continued presence in the US could cause nothing but trouble. The specific event which had prompted them to act was the murder of James Eason, once a senior member of UNIA, who Garvey had expelled. When Eason set up a rival organization called the Universal Negro Alliance, he was killed in New Orleans by two of the UNIA's more fanatical supporters.

The letter compared Garvey's organisation to the Klan, saying it was "just as objectionable and even more dangerous, inasmuch as it naturally attracts an ever lower type of cranks, crooks and racial bigots, among whom suggestibility to violent crime is much greater. The movement known as the Universal Negro Improvement Association has the violent temper of this dangerous element." It then went on to list almost 20 incidents in which it claimed anti-Garvey meetings had been broken up and their speakers attacked. "Garvey, according to the contentions of those who signed the letter, has created an organization which condones and invites crime," said the *Buffalo Courier*. "The attorney general is urged [in the letter] to disband and extirpate this vicious movement and vigorously push the government's case against Marcus Garvey for using the mails to defraud." [2]

Garvey replied with some equally strong language of his own. The Committee of Eight, as the letter's signatories called themselves, were "liars and prevaricators", "Uncle Tom Negroes" and "wicked malingerers" engaged in "the greatest bit of treachery and wickedness that any group of Negroes could be capable of". They were "nearly all Octoroons or Quadroons" or were "married to Octoroons". Pace himself, he said, was interested only in filling his pockets at the expense of the Black people who bought his label's discs. [3]

Garvey was imprisoned on the mail fraud charges then deported to Jamaica in December 1927 – so to that extent I suppose you could say Pace won their little spat. It wouldn't be the last time he heard jibes about his fair skin disqualifying him from being a "real" Black man, though, and his slow-but-steady approach to change would be met with more and more skepticism in the years to come.

# The dying Swan

*"We went into the factory purchase at just the
wrong time, but who could tell it was the wrong
time, at the rate we were making and selling
merchandise then?"*

**- Harry Pace in his October 1925 report to
Black Swan's board.**

*"We were selling around 7,000 records a day
and had only three presses in the factory, which
were making 6,000 records daily, so we were
running behind. We ordered three additional
presses in 1923, made especially for us, and
had them ready for installation. Before they
were set up and ready for running, radio
broadcasting broke and this spelled doom for
us."*

**- Harry Pace in his 1939 letter to Roi Ottley.**

The few hits Black Swan still had to come were achieved
only at the cost of moving even further away from the
release policy Pace had originally wanted.

As late as January 1923, he was still placing ads
lecturing Black readers to pull their socks up and buy some
classical or opera records instead of that awful blues stuff.

One *Crisis* ad announced: "If you – the person reading this advertisement – earnestly want to Do Something for Negro Music, Go to your Record Dealer and ask for the Better Class of Records by Colored Artists". The Black Swan discs listed below included Mrs Antoinette Garnes' soprano rendition of Verdi's *Caro Nome* and Florence Cole-Talbert singing *The Bell Song* from Delibes' *Lakme*. "You will enjoy these," Pace instructed, "and you will Encourage Us to make more and more of this kind of A Record".

He was wrong on both counts. Black Swan's buyers preferred a string of risqué blues songs which the company issued that year: songs like Fae Barnes' *Do It a Long Time, Papa*, Ethel Waters' *You Can't Do What My Last Man Did* and Trixie Smith's *Take It Daddy, It's All Yours*. Another Smith song, *My Man Rocks Me (With One Steady Roll)*, sold well enough to demand several re-pressings. Even so, Black Swan released far fewer "dirty blues" songs than the other labels did, perhaps because Pace found them even more distasteful than the standard blues fare he'd come to rely on.

The 1920s craze for dirty blues had been sparked partly by the record companies' need to offer something the growing medium of radio could not – in this case, good old-fashioned innuendo. But record sales continued to fall, and what little airtime there was available for Black performers was quickly monopolized by Black Swan's bigger competitors. Just like the file-sharing introduced by the likes of Napster in the early 2000s, the new technology of radio gave people their music for free, and no-one wanted to pay for a record when that alternative was available. "Dealers began to cancel orders that they had placed, and records were returned unaccepted," Pace tells Ottley. "We found ourselves making and selling only about 3,000 records daily, then it came down to 1,000 and our factory was closed for two weeks at a time."

A price war broke out among the record companies, eating into everyone's profits but hurting the small labels most of all. Pace, who'd already been forced to cut Black Swan's price from $1 to 85 cents a disc, had to slash it again, this time to just 75 cents. Finally, he was reduced to offering bundles of Black Swan records via mail order, priced at just $7.50 a dozen with a free pack of phonograph needles thrown in.

Meanwhile, Pace's rivals were still doing everything they could to block his distribution channels and poach his remaining artists. "The desire seems to be that we must be put out of business by any means, fair or foul," he told Black Swan's shareholders in July 1923. Victor and Aeolian were proving particularly troublesome, because they both had the financial muscle to force exclusive deals on their distributors. "With the Victor and Aeolian companies, the dealer operates under a franchise and when it is forbidden to sell a record of another make the dealer must and does obey," Pace explains. "During the last three months, as a result of this pressure we have lost some of our very best accounts." [1]

More infuriating still was the unscrupulous way these companies went about trying to tempt Black Swan artists away. Ethel Waters' latest contract with the label, signed on July 8, 1922, included a clause automatically renewing it for another year, providing neither party gave notice to terminate it at least ten days before the contract expired. According to Pace, Aeolian's lawyers encouraged Waters to ignore this clause and to treat the notice requirement as unnecessary. "As a result she recorded for the Aeolian on June 26, even before the 10 day limit," he writes. "Announcement has been made through the trade papers of the proposed issuance of this record and we have served notice on them of the validity of our contract. The matter is in the hands of the attorneys." [2]

Waters responded - again, presumably with Aeolian's encouragement - by suing Pace personally, claiming he still owed her $3,559 of the $6,700 he'd agreed to pay her for her stint on the Troubadours' tour. "This is without foundation of fact and is an endeavor to force a settlement on the Aeolian matter," Pace writes. [3]

It didn't stop with Waters. Here's Pace again:

*"The same tactics have been pursued by the Okeh people, who last week sent an agent to Trixie Smith and endeavored by persuasion and promise of larger payment to have her break her contract with us. Only today another recent singer, Maud DeForest, came in and advised me of the endeavor on the part of the Okeh to have her sing also for them under an assumed name which she refused to do.*

*"Recently a girl called Fae Barnes came here from Dallas, Texas, sent by friends who defrayed her expenses to New York to make records for Black Swan. After we had signed an agreement with her she was picked up by one of the Columbia's colored scouts and we have since been unable to locate her or to have her come in and make the record which she agreed to make."*

It's not clear how the two disputes with Waters were resolved, but we do know that the June 1923 session which produced *Sweet Man Blues* and *Ethel Sings 'Em* was her last for Black Swan. She made a few sides for Paramount in 1924, then settled at Columbia for the next nine years. By the end of 1923, Trixie Smith had left Black Swan too, once again for Paramount. Pace must have found Barnes in the end, because he released her one and only Black Swan record in November 1923, with ads hailing her as "a new star in the firmament of blues singers".

Pace fought back against Black Swan's growing problems in every way he could. Hoping to capitalize on his label's name recognition, he changed Pace Phonograph Corporation's name to The Black Swan Phonograph Company and placed ads in *Crisis* to try and attract new investors. He called on his existing shareholders to pump a little extra cash into the company too, arguing this was the best way to preserve the value of their Black Swan investment in the long term. For the most part, these appeals were ignored – probably because it was only Pace who refused to see Black Swan was already in terminal decline. Even his old friend DuBois was now asking Pace to help him find a buyer for his Black Swan shares and eager to cash in his Fletcher Record Company bond. [4]

Pace cut Black Swan's staff to the bone, slashed his own salary and spent a great deal of time travelling round the US collecting money Black Swan was owed by various distributors and retailers. He let out the space the company no longer needed in its Harlem headquarters to raise some rent there and hired out the Long Island City plant's printing facilities to paying clients. He put his own money into the company with no assurance he'd ever get it back and took on personal debt to help keep it afloat too. But it was no more than a holding operation. In August 1923, Black Swan held its last recording session and, by the end of that year, it had stopped advertising too. The company was effectively in mothballs.

\*\*\*

In January 1924, a white businessman called Maurice Supper boarded a train in Port Washington, Wisconsin. Supper worked for the Wisconsin Chair Company, Paramount Records' parent firm, and he was on his way to

New York to negotiate a deal with Harry Pace which would end in Paramount leasing Black Swan's master discs for re-release. The completed deal was announced in March, with *New York Age* rather improbably describing it as a "merger" between Black Swan and Paramount.

"It is a practical certainty that the Black Swan Co will receive not less than $50,000 for its phonographic interests," the paper continues. "While the deal was in progress, another large competing company got wind of it and approached Pace with a substantial counter offer, but the Wisconsin people promptly met the new offer and clinched it. They take over the good will and trade name, together with the master plates of all the records heretofore made by Black Swan." [5]

Paramount was keen to present this as a means to assure "the continuance of high class race music", topping its *Crisis* ad announcing the move with a photo of Black Swan's Florence Cole-Talbert. "This combination marks the unusual event of a merger of a large Negro company and a large white organization," it added in its 1924 catalogue. "It brings together the two leaders in the Race records field and now makes Paramount, more than ever, the unquestioned leader in the Race records business." [6]

Pace later explained that he'd tried to find an outright buyer for Black Swan, but that the record industry was at such a low ebb none had been able to offer a realistic price. Under the Paramount arrangement, he said, Black Swan would become a holding company rather than an operating company. "The Black Swan catalogue of several hundred master records is the most valuable of its kind in existence," he went on. "Instead of the company operating that catalogue, the Paramount Company will manufacture and distribute Black Swan Records, from which the Black Swan Co will receive a definite amount each month."

The deal gave Paramount access to all of Black Swan's recordings – somewhere between 300 and 350 sides in all - plus its artist contracts, logo rights and goodwill. Starting in May 1924, it began releasing those sides under an imprint which combined both the Paramount and the Black Swan logos. Ethel Waters, Trixie Smith, Katie Crippen and the rest of Black Swan's blues singers were all included, but so too were many of its classical artists. Unfortunately, tastes had already moved on and the records sold poorly. After little more than a year, Pace charged Paramount with defaulting on its monthly leasing payments and took his masters back. [7]

That was effectively Black Swan's last gasp. With the help of his company secretary Pace struggled on for a few months, keeping the firm's admin in order and doing what they could to clear any remaining debts. It was the final days of *Moon Illustrated Weekly* all over again.

By Autumn 1925, even Pace was ready to give up. He clearly felt betrayed by the lack of help – and sometimes downright obstruction – he'd had from Black Swan's other directors and gave vent to those feelings in rather bitter letter to them that October. It's one of those rare Pace documents where he actually gives us a glimpse into his emotions – in this case, disappointment and a growing anger. Here's some extracts:

*"You men ought to know how bitterly disappointed I must have been that Black Swan was not the success I had hoped. You ought also to be honest enough and fair enough to admit that it was no fault of mine. No-one could have foreseen the utter collapse of an industry such as this by some new unheard of discovery like Radio. [...] And yet some have criticized me because I could not make Black Swan pay under such circumstances. Some have said I ought to have*

*stuck to it and made it pay anyway. They attribute to me the ability of a superman, which of course I must modestly deny.*"

"*When the bankruptcy court threatened and when the sheriff was almost a daily visitor, I did not run. I stood my ground and fought it out. I had to discontinue the manufacture of records because it was impossible to sell them. I threw my own meagre personal resources into the breach to save the company. I cut off salaried employees, except one necessary responsible assistant. I gave my own services to collecting its money, paying its bills and managing its affairs.*"

"*During this period, it became necessary to borrow money to save [Black Swan] from bankruptcy. I pledged my own collateral up to the last bond or stock that I owned for its debts. I endorsed notes, jeopardizing my safety and that of my family, in order to protect the investment of its stockholders. And yet, when I appealed to stockholders asking for a loan of just $10 for each share, to bear interest and be returned to them, not a dollar were they willing to risk.*" [8]

And that was more or less that. John Fletcher Records declared bankruptcy and the Long Island City plant was sold at a sheriff's sale to Chicago's Capitol Roll & Record Co, which manufactured discs for Sears & Roebuck. The mortgage lender foreclosed on the Harlem office building and Pace allowed Black Swan's business charter to dissolve. It was over.

*Harry Pace in middle age. Art by Karl Stevens.*

# Afterlives

*"[Armstrong's] legato phrasing, ability to 'tell a story' and use of space for dramatic effect, not to mention his beautiful tone, made a huge impression on the other musicians. By the time Satch went back to Chicago, Fletcher Henderson's big band had evolved from a dance band into the first real swing orchestra."*

**- Scott Yarrow in his sleeve notes to Warner Brothers'** *Louis Armstrong Vol. 5.*

Many of Black Swan's stars went on to great success after the label's demise, with Alberta Hunter starring opposite Paul Robeson in the London premiere of *Showboat* and Ethel Waters scoring a 1949 Oscar nomination for her role in Elia Kazan's *Pinky*. We'll come to Waters in a moment, but first let's talk about Fletcher Henderson, whose contribution in purely musical terms made the biggest mark of all.

After quitting Black Swan in 1923, he formed a New York dance orchestra which quickly won a long residency at the city's prestigious Roseland Ballroom. His only real rival in New York was Paul Whiteman, whose white orchestra ruled that side of the racial divide as firmly as Henderson ruled his own. At one point, Henderson's band was promoted with ads calling him "the colored Paul

Whiteman", and both men thrived by offering a mixture of foxtrots and waltzes for dancing rather than anything we'd recognize as jazz today.

That changed in 1924, when Henderson contacted Louis Armstrong again and repeated the job offer he'd made him two years earlier in New Orleans. Armstrong was based in Chicago now, where he'd had a spell with King Oliver's Band before joining another outfit led by Ollie Powers, but wasn't much enjoying the new gig. Lil Hardin, who he'd married in February that year, had succeeded in focusing his ambition much more sharply, so this time he accepted Henderson's offer and moved to New York in October 1924 to take his place as first cornet in Henderson's dance orchestra. It was this job which gave him his first national showcase, as well as his first chance to sing on stage – but it was his cornet playing which made most impact of all. At one after-hours gig in Harlem a few weeks after joining the orchestra, Armstrong stunned the crowd with something they'd simply never heard before.

"Henderson came out on the stage with his band after finishing for the night at Roseland," Walter Allen writes in *Hendersonia*. "After a suitable warm-up number, he let Armstrong take a solo. Louis Hooper recalled that it was on *What-Cha-Call-'Em Blues* – not a long solo but 'outstanding in style and swing'. As Armstrong took further solos on other tunes, the crowd began to realize this was something special and that, good as Joe Smith had been, they had a new trumpet king of New York now!"

When Henderson and his arranger Don Redman started incorporating Armstrong's freewheeling, improvisational style into their own dance charts, what emerged was the music we now call swing. The seeds of this exciting new music had already been there in what Henderson and Redman were doing, but it took Armstrong's influence and their experience of playing with him to complete the process. "Louis, his style and his feeling, changed our whole idea about the band musically," Redman later said.

Duke Ellington was still in his twenties when he first heard Henderson's orchestra playing these new swing arrangements, and that's the moment that crystalised his own ambitions. But it was Henderson, not Ellington, who made it possible for swing to move from the cognoscenti in a few big city clubs to a truly global phenomenon. In an odd reversal of Black Swan's renaming episode with the old Olympic sides, this time the trick was done by giving Henderson's Black music a white face.

Henderson's orchestra went from strength to strength in the decade following Armstrong's arrival, pulling in top-flight players like Coleman Hawkins, Roy Eldridge and Lester Young. By 1934, though, both Redman and Hawkins had quit, and Henderson was tiring of the pressure involved in running his own outfit. He began selling arrangements to Benny Goodman's orchestra instead – often the very same arrangements the Henderson Orchestra had used - and continued doing so till 1939, when he closed down his own band altogether and joined Goodman's full-time as its first Black arranger and pianist. (1)

As a white musician, Goodman had the regular access to national radio Henderson himself would never have been allowed. It was Goodman's weekly appearances on the NBC radio show *Let's Dance*, combined with a 1935 US tour, which broke swing among America's mainstream white audience. Without Henderson's arrangements, Goodman could never have made the impact he did, and the swing era might never have been born. "Goodman [always credited Henderson], quite justly with providing a very large share of the bedrock on which Benny's early bands stood," says Orrin Keepnews' *Pictorial History of*

*Jazz.* "Fletcher Henderson's arrangements, some based on what his own band had played, were as good a working definition as you could hope to find of what swing is all about." [2]

The two men's partnership was "the uncanny amalgam of success that precipitated the swing era", adds jazz critic Gunther Schuller. "In a number of instances, Goodman took over, virtually intact, the identical arrangements Henderson had already recorded and performed for years. With Henderson, these performances remained virtually unnoticed; with Goodman they became world hits." [3]

None of this could have happened if Black Swan hadn't persuaded Henderson to switch from his dad's uptight music to blues and given him that extra tuition in "damn-it-to-hell" playing which Waters provided. No Black Swan would have meant no Troubadours tour, no opportunity for Henderson to meet the young Louis Armstrong, and hence no Henderson/Redman swing charts either. No Henderson swing charts means no Benny Goodman to take the music from cult favourite to global phenomenon – and without the bands that phenomenon produced, where would singers like Peggy Lee and Frank Sinatra have learned their trade?

* * *

Ethel Waters went on from Black Swan to have a massive career in recording, theatre, film and TV, racking up a great many firsts in the process. As well as being the first Black woman to appear on radio, she was the first to have her name above the title in a Broadway show (*Africana*, 1927), the first to have her own radio series (*The American Revue*, 1933) and TV showcase (*The Ethel Waters Show*, 1939), the first to be nominated for an Emmy (*Route 66*, 1961) and the first to front her own TV sitcom (*Beulah*, 1950). As well as her Oscar-nominated performance in *Pinky*, she starred in filmed versions of several musicals, including *Cabin in the Sky* (1943) and *The Member of the Wedding* (1952). She was also the first professional singer to perform several future jazz classics, including both *Heat Wave* and *Stormy Weather* (both in 1933).

It's an impressive list. But for our purposes, her most interesting project after Black Swan was the 1933 Broadway Revue *As Thousands Cheer,* which contained an anti-lynching song called *Supper Time* Irving Berlin had written especially for her. The only anti-lynching song anyone remembers today is Billie Holiday's *Strange Fruit*, recorded in 1939 from a poem published just two years earlier. What's forgotten is that Waters was performing *Supper Time* on Broadway a full six years before Holiday's *Strange Fruit* was released. Doing that song every night in the show – as Waters did for well over a year – took her straight back to something she'd witnessed at the Douglass Theatre in Macon, Georgia, just a couple of months after the Black Swan Troubadours' gig there.

Waters had returned to the Douglass in August 1922 for a show of her own, this time billed as "Ethel Waters of Black Swan Records" and with just a single pianist to provide her music. The theatre, located between Mulberry and Cherry Streets on what's now Martin Luther King Boulevard, was the focal point of Macon's most important Black neighbourhood, and a big draw for the city's whole African-American community. As Waters knew from her earlier visit, the weekend streets around there would normally be jumping with all the vivacity of a miniature Harlem. Not this time, though: as soon as Waters and her accompanist arrived, they could see something was wrong.

"We sensed something grim and forbidding about

the place," she writes in her autobiography. "The people around the showhouse were the same as usual, except that they didn't say anything. It was as though a sorrow too profound to express hung over them. We weren't there long before we were told the truth. A colored boy had been accused of talking back to a white man. For that he'd been lynched, and the white mob that murdered the youngster had flung his body into the lobby of our theater. They threw it there to make sure many Negroes would see it."

Waters tells us no more about the case than that, but a search of the newspaper archive reveals there's only one Macon incident she can have had in mind – and that's the vigilante murder of John "Cocky" Glover on August 1, 1922. Glover had actually been accused of killing a white cop, something Waters seems not to have been aware of, but he really was murdered by a lynch mob in the cruelest way possible, and the men who did it really did throw his body into the lobby of the Douglass Theatre. I've written a full account of the case elsewhere. [4]

It was memories of Glover's parents which fuelled Waters' performance of *Supper Time*. "As it turned out, the house I was boarding at was next door to the house of that dead boy's family," she writes. "His people told me he was guilty of no crime. He had no trial nor any chance to defend himself. I became friendly with that grief-torn family. I sat with them, prayed with them and tried to comfort them. But what is there to say to the mother of a lynched boy?"

*Supper Time* takes a more oblique approach to its chilling subject than *Strange Fruit* does, but in its way it's just as powerful a song. Berlin's concept for the show was to present 21 songs and sketches drawn from the news of the day, with each one given its context on stage by a backdrop of appropriate headlines. In the case of *Supper Time*, that meant a headline reading "Unknown Negro Lynched by Frenzied Mob", which appeared behind Waters as she walked on from the wings in a cheap housedress and pinny. Her character for the song was a hard-pressed Black mother, still reeling from the news that her innocent husband has just been lynched. As she struggles to prepare her children's evening meal, she wonders how she's going to tell them that they'll never see their father again and – harder yet – how to preserve both their faith and her own in a merciful God. "How can I remind them to pray at their humble board?" Berlin has her ask. "How can I be thankful when they start to thank the Lord?"

Audiences were visibly moved by Waters' performance of this song and often as not it stopped the show. Carol Channing, then just 12 years old, was in the audience one night and never forgot what she'd seen. "Ethel Waters, this monumental woman, had a bandana on her head, she had an apron on," Channing told PBS in 2012. "Behind her was the silhouette of a man hanging from a tree, with his head on the side, with a rope around his neck. We didn't know in those days about lynchings in the South. She came forward with the beat of that orchestra, and she went into it." And here's Channing again, this time describing Waters' performance of the song to the *New York Post* in 1969: "[As she] moved slowly down to the footlights, my heart started to pound. When she began to sing, I got so thrilled it was embarrassing. I looked at Ethel Waters and lost my breath." [5, 6]

For Waters herself, this number was far more than just a piece of entertainment. "If one song can tell the whole tragic history of a race, *Supper Time* was that song," she wrote years later. "In singing it, I was telling my comfortable, well-fed, well-dressed listeners about my people. I had only to think of the family of that boy down in Macon, Georgia, to give adequate expression to the horror and defeat."

\*\*\*

After Pace shuttered Black Swan, he returned to the finance industry. In 1925 he persuaded Solvent and a number of other Black-owned banks to finance him in setting up a new insurance company called Northeastern Life, which Pace ran as president. The company specialised in providing insurance for Black customers, who'd often be turned away elsewhere. Four years later, and now based in Chicago, he drove through a three-way merger bringing Northeastern together with Supreme Life and Liberty Life, the two other major insurers then serving African-Americans. The 1929 merger created a company called Supreme Liberty Life, which had $25m worth of insurance in force, total assets of $1.4m and over 1,000 employees. Pace was appointed its president and chief executive.

In 1930, he decided the time had finally come to get the law degree he'd wanted ever since those ambitions were derailed by DuBois' offer of a job on *Moon Illustrated Weekly*. He told none of his friends or colleagues about this, but quietly enrolled at Chicago Law School. "For a period of three years, after working hours, and for a long time unknown to even his closest associates, Pace spent four nights a week in law school or in the library of the law institute," the *Chicago Defender* reported on his graduation in 1933. "Ranking fourth in a class of 41 graduates, four others of whom were Colored, Mr Pace received the degree of doctor of jurisprudence cum laude and was one of seven members of the class elected to the honorary law school fraternity, the Order of Lincoln". Soon after graduating, he became a partner in the Chicago law practice Bibb, Tyree & Pace, but retained his job at Supreme Liberty Life too. [7]

Pace would regularly attend meetings of Chicago's Urban League, an organisation devoted to improving Black people's lot in the city, and that's where he met a bright young student called John Johnson, later to become a publishing magnate with magazines like *Ebony* and *Jet*. Johnson had come to the meeting to hear Pace's speech that night and managed to corner him for a moment afterwards to say how much he'd enjoyed it. Pace asked the 18-year-old Johnson what he planned to do with his life, and Johnson replied that he'd been offered a scholarship at the University of Chicago but was going to have to turn it down because he had no means of supporting himself there. Pace saved the day by immediately offering him a part-time job at Supreme Liberty Life.

Johnson started working there in September 1936, first as an office boy and then as Pace's own assistant, and it was during this period that he had the idea for his first magazine, *Negro Digest*. One of his duties at the company was to clip articles from the Black press and present his selection of these to Pace once a month for possible inclusion in the company's house magazine. Whenever Johnson discussed the articles he'd found with friends or family members, they were always interested, and always keen to know where they could find a copy for themselves. He realised there was a gap in the market for a Black version of *Readers' Digest* – a monthly magazine which compiled or summarized every article of interest that had appeared in the Black press over the previous few weeks.

Pace, who seems to have seen something of himself in the young man, helped push this idea along in every way he could. He told Johnson all about his own early experience in journalism, gave him a lot of valuable business advice and even let him use Supreme Liberty Life's mailing list to recruit *Negro Digest's* first subscribers. Johnson published the first issue in 1942, quit the insurer a year later, and never looked back. "[Pace] definitely was my mentor," he later said. "My real school from 1936 till 1941 was the University of Supreme Life." [8, 9]

# Hansberry v Lee

*"That fight required that our family occupy the
disputed property in a hellishly hostile white
neighborhood in which literally howling mobs
surrounded our house. One of [their] missiles
almost took the life of the eight-year-old signer
of this letter. [...] I also remember my
desperate and courageous mother patrolling
our household all night with a loaded German
luger, doggedly guarding her four children."*

**- Lorraine Hansberry in an unpublished
letter to the *New York Times*.**

Even after all Pace's success, race never ceased to be an
issue for him. Chicago's Black population had grown
eightfold since the turn of the century, but many all-white
neighbourhoods still resisted the idea of even a single
Black family moving in. Once, they'd used home-made
bombs to scare any Black incomers into moving out again
pretty quickly, but by the mid-1930s they preferred to rely
on restrictive covenants. In one particular white Chicago
neighbourhood called Woodlawn, for example, there was a
covenant in place barring homeowners from selling or
renting their properties to anyone with the merest drop of
Black blood.

Pace believed covenants like these were
unconstitutional and, in April 1937, he came up with a plan
to put that belief to the test. He identified a house for sale

on Woodlawn's East 60th Street, which runs along the southern edge of Washington Park, and recruited a white man called James Burke to help him buy it. Burke was a former officer of the Woodlawn Property Owners' Association, which had drawn up the restrictive covenant in the first place, but had fallen out with the other members and flounced off swearing to get his revenge by putting a black family on every block there. [1, 2]

The house Pace had his eye on was owned by Walter and May Harrower, a white couple who'd signed the restrictive covenant and already turned down a generous offer from one Black applicant. The house had been on the market for over a year, but still they refused to sell or rent it to anyone Black. Burke told Walter Harrower he'd found a white buyer for him, a wholesale clothier called Henry Lutz, and Lutz bought the house on April 14, 1937. That was clearly a part of Pace's scheme too, because Lutz immediately sold the house on to Edward and Aeolian Parrish, a New York couple related to Pace's wife Ethlynde. They used a Supreme Liberty Life mortgage, arranged by Pace, to give them the purchase price.

Two weeks later, on April 29, Pace leased the house from the Parrishes and, 18 days after that, he bought it outright and moved his family in. Census data shows they were still living there in 1940. The plan had worked like clockwork and given the Paces a nice house into the bargain – but it was really just a dry run for what he had in mind next.

\*\*\*

In May 1937, Pace joined forces with Carl Hansberry, a savvy Black Chicago real estate broker and political activist, to buy another Woodlawn house – this one at 6140

South Rhodes Avenue. Helped by the NAACP, they hoped to provoke a court case which would challenge the whole legality of segregated housing. Once again, Burke agreed to help.

The Rhodes Avenue house was owned by First National Bank of Englewood. Burke approached them saying that, in return for some commission on the sale, he could find them a suitable white buyer, and the bank agreed. A week later, he returned with a white buyer called Jay Crook who, it later emerged, knew the Hansberrys. Crook bought the house for $6,500, that money again coming from a Supreme Liberty Life mortgage. He immediately sold it on to Carl Hansberry for $7,000, giving Crook the $500 profit which was presumably his price for taking part in the plan. Burke got his commission from the bank, so he was happy too. Carl Hansberry and his family – including the eight-year-old Lorraine – moved in.

When the neighbourhood's white property owners realised they'd been tricked they launched a campaign of vicious harassment against the Hansberrys, using all the thuggish tactics Lorraine Hansberry describes in the quote topping this chapter. Her sister Mamie later gave an interview to the *Chicago Tribune* saying the missile which had narrowly missed Lorraine's head was a chunk of concrete, hurled with such force that it smashed through a closed window and embedded itself in the room's interior wall. "My memories of this 'correct' way of fighting white supremacy in America include being spat at, cursed and pummeled in the daily trek to and from school," Lorraine herself told the *New York Times*. [3, 4]

While all this was going on, the Woodlawn property owners were preparing a legal challenge. This effort was led by Anna Lee, one of WPOA's more hard-line members, who accused Pace and Hansberry of a conspiracy to subvert the restrictive covenant. She demanded $100,000 in restitution, knowing a sum that size would force them both to sell their houses and move out to meet the fine. Pace enlisted Earl Dickerson, a very talented Black lawyer who also held the post of Supreme Liberty Life's corporate attorney, to defend himself and Hansberry in court. This would be the test case he'd hoped to provoke all along. [5]

Hansberry v Lee began its long progress through the courts in March 1938, with both Pace and Supreme Liberty Life named as Carl Hansberry's co-defendants. The circuit court in Illinois' Cook County heard it first, where Pace faced some hostile questioning from the WPOA's lawyer Charles Churan:

> **Churan:** *"Pardon me asking you this, Mr Pace. You are a Negro, are you not?"*
>
> **Pace:** *"Well, that would be a conclusion on my part. I am commonly known as a colored person. You can form your own conclusion, please."*
>
> **Churan:** *"Well, I mean, you admit that you are ..."*
>
> **Pace:** *"I say I am commonly known as a colored man and prefer to be known as such."*

It's easy to see what Churan was up to here. He wanted to underline that the fair-skinned, well-dressed and well-spoken Pace was, in the eyes of the law, Black – and hence barred by the restrictive covenant from living in Woodlawn. But Pace's response is much harder to interpret. Should we read it as a proud declaration of his racial identity? Or simply as a statement that he prefers the term "colored man" to "Negro"? We'll return to this point in the next chapter, so just file the thought away for now.

Cook County's decision went in favour of the WPOA, but Dickerson pressed on with an appeal to the

Illinois Supreme Court. That appeal confirmed the lower court's decision, forcing the Hansberrys to temporarily move out of Rhodes Avenue while they waited for a further appeal to the US Supreme Court to be heard. That took a while, but, finally, on November 13, 1940, SCOTUS was ready to announce its verdict. It overturned both the previous courts' rulings, declaring that the Woodlawn restrictive covenants were void, and so could not be enforced in any way. It reached this decision on a technicality of the covenants themselves rather than the bedrock constitutional principle Pace and Hansberry had hoped to establish, but a win was still a win.

The case had rested on the WPOA's own terms in its restrictive covenant stating that 95% of homeowners there must sign it in order to make the covenant valid. When launching their action, they'd claimed in court that 98% had actually signed the thing, but Dickerson proved that the true figure was only 54%. You can't enforce a covenant that was never valid in the first place, so SCOTUS ruled the Hansberrys' purchase could stand. Prior to this decision, bodies like the WPOA had only needed to cite the precedent of an earlier covenants case called Burke v Kleiman to rack up an automatic win. The Hansberrys' victory meant that precedent could no longer be relied on, which dramatically increased both the risk of suing Black buyers over such covenants and the cost of doing so. These were significant disincentives for anyone with the WPOA's views.

Hansberry v Lee certainly didn't end Chicago's segregated housing, but it was important as the first domino to fall. The immediate effect was to free up hundreds of homes in what had previously been the city's all-white neighbourhoods. "Hansberry Decision Opens 500 New Homes to Negroes," the jubilant *Chicago Defender* reported. From that point on, restrictive covenants were a busted flush, not only in Woodlawn, but throughout the city.

Eight years later, the 1948 case of Shelley v Kraemer finished the job Pace had begun, establishing conclusively that racial covenants breached Black people's 14th amendment rights to equal protection under the law. Lorraine Hansberry, the little girl who'd found herself dodging concrete missiles in Rhodes Avenue, retold the story in her 1959 Broadway play *A Raisin in the Sun*, which was later filmed with Sidney Poitier and made the real house so famous it's now an official Chicago landmark. [6]

# Burying a secret

*"Pace was so light you'd bever believe he was Black unless he told you. His whole family, in fact, was light-skinned and there were rumors, never substantiated, that his children were passing for white."*

**- John Johnson in his 1989 autobiography *Succeeding Against the Odds.***

*"He was very fair-skinned, but he identified completely with Blacks until he had a daughter and a son who went to the University of Wisconsin. They fell in love with white boys and girls, and they wanted to get married. The time came for them to meet the parents, and naturally they didn't want to meet a Black person."*

**- John Johnson in his National Visionary Leadership Project interview (2002).**

Something strange happened in the Pace household in the 1930s, evidence of which appears in the family's US census data. The census form then included a question demanding to know the "color or race" of everyone living in the house. For the Paces, that meant Harry, Ethlynde, their two children (Harry Jr and Josephine) plus a live-in maid called Catherine Black. They're entered . as "Neg" for "Negro" in all five cases. Fast-forward to the next census, held in 1940, and everything's changed. The maid's no longer there, but the four family members are still under the same roof – and this time they're all described as "W" for white. [1]

The Johnson quotes above give us some useful background here. Harry Jr and Josephine were both now students at the University of Wisconsin and had been presenting as white while there. American kids normally go to college at around 17, an age which Harry Jr reached in 1935 and Josephine in 1938, so the timing's a good match for the data we have on the census forms. Harry and Ethlynde had always been light-skinned enough to present as white if they'd chosen to do so, but now the census data made it official. Harry's comments in that Illinois courtroom about preferring to be known as "a colored man" – which came at the same time all this was playing out – tell us he must have been at least a little conflicted about the change. [2]

There was a second factor too. In around 1942, Harry moved the family to another white Chicago suburb called River Forest, reigniting Garvey's old charge that he was nothing but an Uncle Tom. One group of Supreme Liberty Life employees were so incensed by this that they drew up plans to follow Pace home one night and demonstrate outside his house in order to embarrass him in front of his white neighbours. According to Johnson, when Pace heard about the plan he went through a personality change:

*"I went to Pace and told him what people were saying and what they intended to do. Pace didn't deny the reports. He thanked me, got his hat and went out the*

*back door, leaving his car as a subterfuge. From that day till his death a year later, he was a changed man, more cautious, more withdrawn, more secretive. He took taxis and buses to different commuter stations and he stopped taking home his usual armful of Black newspapers and periodicals."* [(3)]

There's evidence of this new, shrunken Harry Pace in a *New York Age* story which appeared in July 1943. "Friends from New York who visited Chicago in recent months said they had visited the offices of the insurance company and been informed that the insurance company president [Pace] was ill," it says of Supreme Liberty Life. "Efforts to learn of his home address were likewise futile, it being said that not even employees of the company were aware of the new address of their chief executive. All personal mail for Mr Pace, it was said, was sent to the insurance company office, and was called for personally by Mr Pace's wife, who visited the office periodically to get his mail and his salary cheques." [(4)]

Harry Pace died at 196 South Delaplaine Road in Chicago on July 19, 1943, aged just 59. That's in a different part of the city to both Woodlawn and River Forest, which suggests Harry had taken the threat of protests at River Forest seriously enough to move his family out to a new location which they were careful never to reveal. Josephine Pace provided the information for her father's death certificate, giving his race there as "white" and his occupation as "lawyer". But there was one more twist to come.

\*\*\*

On July 31, 1943 – nearly two weeks after Harry had passed – *New York Age* carried a front page story reporting his demise. "Body shipped here for quiet funeral," its headline read. "Secrecy surrounds death." The tone of the story beneath is one of shock, anger and disappointment. Here's some extracts:

*"Eastern and mid-western societies and business leaders of the nation were shocked this week to learn of the death at his home of Harry H. Pace, president of the the Supreme Liberty Life Insurance Company, and a noted lawyer of Chicago, Illinois. But what shocked them even more was the fact that his body was shipped east to New York City and buried quietly before even his closest New York friends and associates were aware of the fact that he was dead."*

*"Almost as soon as word reached them that the noted insurance executive was dead, some of his friends began speculating as to why such secrecy should have surrounded the death and burial of so prominent a national figure. It has been rumored for some time that Mr Pace had been in ill health and had been inactive in his office in the Supreme Liberty Life Insurance Company in Chicago and at the law firm of Bibb, Tyree and Pace, but no-one was aware of the nature of his illness or why such secrecy should have surrounded the fact that he was ill."*

*"From other close friends, it was reported that perhaps the reason for the secrecy was due to the fact that his two children, a son, Harry Jr, and daughter Josephine, were said to be 'passing' for white and therefore were anxious to cut off all ties with Negroes.*

*The son was said to have entered the army as 'white'.*

"*Whatever the reason for the secrecy, members of the family could not be reached for comment, either by members of the press or by Mr Pace's oldest friends who had learned of the death by rumors. One prominent Harlemite in particular, a friend of Mr Pace for 39 years, was not notified of his death and learned of it only by accident. He was particularly bitter over the fact that he did not even have the chance to take a last look at or pay homage to his old friend, who he had come to regard 'as a brother'.*" [5]

There's really only one construction you can put on this: Pace's wife and children were so determined to conceal his Black identity that they rushed his body to New York for a secret burial, denying even his closest friends the chance to say goodbye. It was a sad end to such a packed and remarkable life. [6]

\*\*\*

I first stumbled on the Black Swan story in 2007 while researching a BBC radio documentary on a different aspect of 1920s blues. There was no room for the Black Swan material in that programme, though, so I stuck it in a file and continued researching the label on and off for the next 18 months. I first wrote about it in a 2009 essay for my website PlanetSlade.com, and I've been slowly adding to my knowledge about Pace and his label ever since. [7]

A few months after the website piece appeared, I got a letter from Harry's grand-daughter, Susan Pace Hoy, confirming that her father, Harry Jr, had taken the family's secret to his grave. "We never knew anything of our father's family," she told me. "I was raised as white and never knew anything different until 2007, when a family member discovered Jitu K. Weusi's essay *The Rise and Fall of Black Swan Records*.

"Through a friend I was able to speak with Lerone Bennett Jr, who co-authored John Johnson's book. He told me that Johnson expressed regrets that Pace's children and grandchildren were 'lost' to the tradition and would never know the trials, challenges and triumphs of a great American story. It has been a rollercoaster ride these past two years with this discovery and I am still trying to put all of the pieces together. I am grateful that I finally know the secrets that my family has kept buried for so long." [8, 9]

# Postscript

*"Ladies and gentlemen, if I seem to take special pride in presenting our next guest it's because it really is an honor to be appearing with her on the* Hollywood Palace *tonight. Miss Waters and I never met till this week, and for me this is a showbusiness legend come to life."*

**- Diana Ross introducing Waters on a 1969 TV show.**

In March 1969, Diana Ross hosted an edition of the ABC network variety show *Hollywood Palace*. As one of her guests she chose Ethel Waters, who sang *Supper Time* on the show after sharing a duet with Ross on Hoagy Carmichael's *Bread & Gravy*.

For Waters, it must have been a strange experience. In Black Swan's heyday she'd been just as big a star as Ross was now, and just as important as her label's single most defining face. "When I began in show business at the age of 17, I was known as Sweet Mama Stringbean," she ruefully remarked, glancing down at Ross's skinny form. "Now I'm shaped more like a brussel sprout."

*Diana Ross with Ethel Waters on 1969's*
Hollywood Palace *TV show.*

# Sources and endnotes

### Exceptional men.

1) *History of the American Negro and his Institutions: Georgia Edition,* ed. Arthur Caldwell (AB Caldwell, 1917).

2) Rape was a crime very commonly inflicted by white slaveowners on their Black female slaves in the US. A December 2020 *New Yorker* piece by Douglas Preston explains that African-Americans have, on average, about 80% African DNA and 20% European. "But about 80% of that European ancestry is inherited from white males – genetic testimony to the widespread rape and sexual coercion of female slaves by slaveowners," he adds.

3) Both Pace and Caldwell were living in Atlanta as Caldwell worked on his book, so it's perfectly possible that they knew each other. My guess is that the signed photo of Pace accompanying the profile in Caldwell's book was a gift directly from him to the author, and that he provided all his own biographical details too.

4) *The Man Who Won* appeared in the April and May 1913 issues of WEB DuBois' *Crisis* magazine.

5) *Memphis Blues* was serialised in the *Chicago Defender,* which ran it in 14 weekly installments between July 7, 1934 and October 6 the same year.

6) We use the phrase "sold down the river" to describe any kind of betrayal now, but in the slavery era it had a far more specific meaning. To be sold down the river then meant you'd been bought by an owner further south along the Mississippi, and the further down the river this transaction took you, the more cruel the treatment you were likely to find there.

7) DuBois' *Talented Tenth* essay first appeared in a collection called *The Negro Problem* (J. Pott & Co, 1903). The book's other contributors include Booker T. Washington and the poet Paul Laurence Dunbar.

**Man on the *Moon*.**

1) Letters from DuBois to the banker Jacob Schiff, dated April 4, 1905 and January 19, 1906. Like the other DuBois letters quoted here, they can be found online in the University of Massachusetts Amherst's Credo archive.
2) Letter from DuBois to Pace. He gives no date on the letter, but it seems to have been written in March or April 1905.
3) The figure usually given here is $3,000 between them, but it's not clear how much of that went specifically to the *Moon* and how much to the print shop's general funding. Simon claims in a 1907 letter to DuBois that Pace's cash investment in the business was only $300.
4) The magazine had a second salesman making similar calls in Atlanta. Advertisers there included Alonzo Herndon's Atlanta Mutual Insurance, Dr FB Badger ("Atlanta's first Black dentist") and The People's Shoe Store ("The only first class shoe store in the city owned by colored people").
5) *The Moon Illustrated Weekly: Black America's First Weekly Magazine*, by Paul Partington (Paul G Partington, 1986).
6) *Beale Street: Where the Blues Began,* by George W Lee (McGrath Publishing Co, 1934).
7) *DuBois' Memphis Connection,* by Miriam DeCosta-Willis (West Tennessee Historical Society Papers volume 42, 1988).
8) *New York Age,* August 2, 1906.
9) These letters from Simon to DuBois are dated December 22, 1906 and January 30, 1907 respectively.
10)     Letter from Pace to DuBois, February 13, 1907.
11)     *An Economic Detour: A History of Insurance in the Lives of American Negroes*, by Merah Steven Stuart (Wendell Malliet & Co, 1940). My description of Pace's encounter with Ware and the messenger boy is based on Stuart's account too.
12)     Letter from Pace to DuBois, August 21, 1907.
13)     Pace was required to provide a $10,000 bond in order to qualify for the Solvent board – not an easy task for someone of his means. All the white-owned surety companies but one immediately turned him away simply because of his race. In January 1908, he managed to persuade the National Surety Company to take his business, but even their bond came at the price of a higher premium than any equivalent white customer would have been asked to pay.

## Father of the blues.

1) *Father of the Blues*, by WC Handy (Macmillan, 1944).
2) The initials of Mississippi's Yazoo-Delta rail line led to it being nicknamed the "Yellow Dog". The YD intersected with the Southern rail line at a junction called Moorhead, and that's the spot identified in the song: "Where the Southern cross the Dog".
3) What Handy's describing here, of course, is a man playing slide guitar.
4) Sheet music sales still dominated the industry at this point. Record sales would not surpass them till the 1920s.
5) *Long Lost Blues: Popular Blues in America, 1850-1920*, by Peter Muir (University of Illinois, 2010).
6) Letter from Handy to the blues writer Abbe Niles. Quoted in *Ramblin' On My Mind: New Perspectives on the Blues,* by David Evans (University of Illinois, 2008). "Song sharks were publishers who took fees from songwriters to publish songs that they never promoted or distributed," Evans writes. "These con men were a common scourge in the early decades of the twentieth century."
7) Peter Muir (above) contrasts a pair of 1913 songs: Pace's *The Girl You Never Have Met* and Handy's *Jogo Blues*. "The two songs represent opposite poles of Handy's creativity," he writes. "*The Girl You Never Have Met* is as musically unadventurous as *Jogo Blues* is experimental."
8) *WC Handy & the Birth of the Blues* (New York Festival of Song, November 2018, programme notes), by Elliott Hurwitt.

## Pace & Handy Inc.

1) P&H had a brief spell in Chicago between their Memphis and New York incarnations. Handy had already moved his family there when Pace suggested the New York move and everything changed again.
2) These sessions took place in September 1917 and were credited to "Handy's Orchestra". The tunes recorded include *Preparedness Blues, The Snaky Blues, Moonlight Blues, The Honking Cow Blues, The Coburn Blues, A Bunch of Blues, Those Draftin' Blues* and *Livery Stable Blues*.
3) Handy adds that both King Edward VIII and the Queen Mother were big fans of *St Louis Blues* when young. He also quotes a press report that Edward had his bagpipers play it for Wallis Simpson during a trip to Balmoral.

4) Pace himself was elected to the NAACP's national board in 1923.


**Too much money.**

1) Ottley prints this letter in his 1969 book *The Negro in New York: An informal social history* (Praeger Paperbacks, 1969).

2) William Kenney's 1993 book *Chicago Jazz: A Cultural History* points out that the record industry at this time was happily targeting every other minority group it could think of. "Decisions to produce black jazz band music on records produced for sale in African-American neighborhoods followed earlier efforts to profit from the sale of Irish, Yiddish, German, French, Native American, Hawaiian, Mexican, Bohemian, Polish, Tyrolean and Scandinavian musics wherever these immigrant groups clustered," he writes.

3) I say "signed" here, but it's not necessarily a full-blown record contract we should imagine. Often, musicians of this era were paid a small one-off fee for recording a song and would never see another cent from it no matter how well the record sold. Long-term contracts and royalty payments entered the picture only when a label was keen to lock in one of its proven stars.


**The first blues record.**

1) The distinction between cabaret (or "classic") blues and its country cousin is well described by the music journalist Jas Obrecht in a piece for his Music Archive website. "[The stars of cabaret blues were] the glittering, glamorous and savvy veterans of tent shows, minstrel troupes and the vaudeville stage," he writes. "Their lyrics were often erotic, frank and cynical. Singers bedecked themselves in sumptuous gowns and paid careful attention to diction while belting out their woes to the accompaniment of a hot jazz ensemble. Whereas country blues singers could string together random verses as long as they wanted, most classic blueswomen relied on stately tunes by successful songwriters such as Clarence Williams, Porter Grainger and the wily Perry Bradford." (Source: https://jobrecht.wordpress.com.)

2) The Hunter incident happened around 1917 when she was singing at a gangster-owned Chicago joint called The Burnham Inn. "One night the lights went out at the inn while she was singing," Frank Taylor writes in his Hunter biography. "Bang. When the lights came back on, a guy was lying dead

by the piano at Alberta's feet." (*Alberta Hunter: A Celebration in Blues* – McGraw-Hill, 1987.)

3) Bert Williams, one of the very few Black artists the majors were prepared to accept, was racking up some big hits for Columbia at this time. His 1919 recording of *The Moon Shines on the Moonshine* shipped 246,000 copies for the company. "This was an impressive figure," says Allan Sutton in his book *Race Records & the American Recording Industry* (Mainstream Press, 2016). "Many releases sold a tenth of that amount and sales of 500 copies represented the break-even point."

4) Bradford later claimed he'd played piano on the disc himself, pulling in Willie Smith only for the publicity photos.

5) Noble Sissle & Eubie Blake – two Black men – retained Smith's "shoot myself a cop" line in their 1927 cover of the song. I'm always slightly surprised they felt safe to do so in that era.

6) White blues fans were also buying *Crazy Blues*. "That record turned round the recording industry," says Danny Barker, a jazz musician who began his career in 1920s New Orleans. "There was a great appeal among Black people and white people who loved this blues business to buy records and buy phonographs." (Source: Jas Obrecht Music Archive).

7) I interviewed Hamilton for a BBC radio project in March 2007.

## Piano man.

1) *The Uncrowned King of Swing: Fletcher Henderson & Big Band Jazz*, by Jeffrey Magee (Oxford University Press, 2005).

## Black Swan rising.

1) Paul Robeson, then a student at Rutgers, spent one summer working at P&H. He then went on to Columbia University, where Pace recruited him in 1921 to moonlight on the Black Swan salesforce. His first recordings wouldn't come till four years later though, and those were for Victor.

2) This story appeared in the paper's February 26, 1921 issue under the headline "Record Co.'s Object To Colored Men Making Phonograph Records". It claimed the Black Swan announcement had been leaked to Pace's white rivals "by certain colored men desirous of starting such trouble", but what lies behind that charge I have no idea.

3) With help from his family – particularly his brother Charles – Handy would eventually manage to salvage both the business and his health.

4) My guess is that the Southern holdings Pace refers to here were employee shares he'd retained from his stints at Solvent in Memphis and Standard Life in Atlanta.

5) Was it simple discretion that had prevented Pace mentioning Williams' backing before? Or was he running the ad now only because he knew Williams could no longer dispute any claim it made? My money's on the latter.

6) Greenfield's own nickname was inspired by Jenny Lind's billing as "The Swedish Nightingale".

7) *Black Swan: The Record Label of the Harlem Renaissance*, by Helge Thygesen, Mark Berresford and Russ Shor (VJM Publications, 1996). This quote comes from the book's introductory essay, which was written by Berresford and Shor alone.

8) The AEF (American Expeditionary Force) fought on the Western Front in World War One under the command of General Pershing.

9) Swanola models available included the Dunbar (named for the pioneering African-American poet Paul Laurence Dunbar) and the L'Ouverture (named for the Haitian revolutionary Toussaint L'Ouverture).

10)   The issue dates here are June 18, 1921 (*New York Age*), February 1921 (*Crisis*) and May 6, 1921 (*Black Dispatch*).

11)   Black Swan would release well over 300 sides before it was done, compared to Broome's output of fewer than a dozen.

12)   *Richmond Planet*, April 29, 1922.

13)   Letter from Still to Walter Allen, 1963. Allen quotes it in *Hendersonia*.

14)   The Smith story's been repeated ad infinitum – often by me – but its prime source seems to be a 1948 letter from Handy to AR Tomlinson, which Sutton quotes in his book. "Bessie Smith's first test record was made by the Black Swan Record Company," Handy writes. "While she was singing she said 'Hold on, let me spit,' and the president [Pace] turned down this celebrity, who became Queen of the Blues on Columbia Records."

15)   Some of Pace's distributors used the "racial uplift" angle in their own ads too. In May 1921, Oklahoma City's Osborne

Bros. Music Co listed Black Swan's first three releases in a *Black Dispatch* ad, saying: "I feel that it is your duty to add one of each number to your cabinet".

16)     One of Pace's outlets was the Nails brothers' shoe store in Tulsa's Greenwood Avenue, a prosperous African-American neighbourhood known as The Black Wall Street. Their shop was destroyed by murderous white rioters in the Tulsa Massacre of May 1921. I don't know if the owners, James and Henry Nails, survived that terrible night or not.

17)     Pace even tried to persuade a few Black preachers to display the label's religious discs at the back of their churches. That was one area where his entreaties fell on stony ground.

18)     The sales figure here of $674.64, which relates to February 1921, is taken from a *New York Age* report of January 28, 1922.


## Sweet Mama Stringbean.

1) *His Eye is on the Sparrow*, by Ethel Waters (Da Capo Press reprint, 1992).

2) What maternal love there was in Ethel's childhood seems to have come from Sally, her grandmother, who was forced to spend most of her time working a string of menial jobs outside the house. Throughout Waters' book, she reserves the warmth of the word "Mom" for Sally alone. Louise gets a chilly "mother" at best and is more often "Momweeze".

3) Waters was billed as Baby Star at the church show, and the old folk song she chose to sing there was almost painfully on-the-nose. "I'm dying for someone to love me," it goes. "Someone to call my own / Someone to stay with me all of my life / For I'm tired of living alone."

4) Louise's signature on this document causes confusion even today. Whenever you see a claim Waters was born in 1896 rather than 1900, this is what lies at the bottom of it.

5) *Jazz From the Beginning*, by Garvin Bushell (Da Capo, 1998).

6) *All-Night Party: The Women of Bohemian Greenwich Village & Harlem,* by Andrea Barnet (Algonquin Books, 2004).

7) Waters' accusation was that Braxton & Nugent earned an extra $25 a night from her participation in the show but continued to pay her only the $10 a night they'd originally agreed. She didn't deny they were entitled to some share of the coins people threw to her onstage as tips, but believed

they were conning her on the split too.

8) Smith had good reason to view Decatur Street as her own territory. She'd begun her professional showbiz career there in 1913, having moved to Atlanta from Tennessee four years earlier.

9) Waters' fellow performers at Edmonds included One-Leg Shadow, a crippled piano player who'd known her father, and Edna Winston, a dancer. Winston's signature routine was the "show your laundry" dance, choreographed to let her repeatedly flash her knickers at the audience.

10)     These were the overnight shifts that Waters would later describe as running "from nine till unconscious". She'd play three or four of her own sets in the course of the night, taking turns with the other performers as she describes.

11)     This description of Williams appeared in *New York Age* on June 3, 1922.

12)     Waters' world did not share our own obsession with giving every individual's sexuality a firm label, and my impression is that she simply saw the boy/girl distinction as nothing to make a great fuss about. She'd always have some man in her life, and she even married a few of them, but frequently launched into same-sex relationships too. Many of her rival cabaret blues stars had female lovers too – Bessie Smith, Alberta Hunter, Ma Rainey – some treating this preference as an unshakable policy and others as a line to be crossed back and forth at will.

13)     *Heat Wave: The Life and Career of Ethel Waters*, by Donald Bogle (Harper Perennial, 2011).

14)     Welch was about the same age as Waters and building her own singing career in many of the same venues. Her quote here appears in Stephen Bourne's book *Elisabeth Welch: Soft Lights and Sweet Music* (Scarecrow Press, 2005).

15)     I've taken Hampton's quote from Cookie Woolner's paper *Ethel Must Not Marry: Black Swan Records & the Queer Classic Blues Women* (International Association for the Study of Popular Music conference, 2012).

16)     In September 1923, rumours swept Harlem that Waters had murdered Williams in Los Angeles during one of their legendary rows. In fact, the victim was a druggy white cabaret dancer called Ethel Williams, who was bludgeoned to death in LA while our two Ethels were playing a show together in Alabama. The fact that Harlem was so ready to believe the

original rumour speaks volumes about the volatility of the Waters/Williams relationship.

### Their first big hit.

1) *Jazz Monthly*, December 1957. Other sources place Edmond's on 130$^{th}$ or 132$^{nd}$ Street. The only thing everyone seems agreed on is that it was somewhere in the 130s.
2) Notice here that, even as late as 1950, when she wrote her book, Waters thinks Handy was a founding partner in Black Swan. That's testimony to how widely and deeply this belief was held, no matter how many times Handy explained it simply wasn't true.
3) Kenney's *Chicago Jazz* (above) has some information on what musicians were then paid. "Sidemen were paid $30 for each master that was cut and approved for production," he writes. "At a time when they often earned from $45 to $75 a week in dance halls and concerts, recording fees could amount to more than wages."
4) Pace had a habit of inflating Black Swan's record sales whenever there was the prospect of some publicity. In June 1921, he wrote to DuBois claiming Black Swan had sold 10,300 records in its first 30 days and asking him to use this snippet in *Crisis*. That figure's hard to reconcile with the modest sales income we see reported for Black Swan elsewhere. DuBois had no reason to doubt it at the time, though, and duly reports the 10,300 claim in the magazine's August 1921 issue.
5) The cash figures here are taken from a *New York Age* story of January 28, 1922, and a letter Pace wrote to DuBois in April that year.
6) The foreign markets Pace was reaching included the West Indies, Central America and the Philippines.
7) One of those agents was Elijah McNeill, who recruited a sub-agent called Walter Caldwell to help him sell Black Swan records in Bridgewater, New Jersey. In October 1921, the two men fell out over a sum of $3.60 which McNeill claimed Caldwell owed him for the records he'd supplied. When this row escalated, he shot Caldwell dead, turned himself in and was convicted of second degree murder. The judge gave him a term of up to 30 years in State prison.
8) Everyone in the band seems to have known the baritone sax player only as "Bill DC". If anyone's aware of his real surname, I've never seen it reported.

9) Henderson wasn't the only band member here to make a big career for himself in jazz. Bushell would later record with Ella Fitzgerald, John Coltrane and Gil Evans, while Gus Aiken later recorded with both Louis Armstrong and Sidney Bechet.

10)    This "parable" (as he calls it) is described in Magee's book and dated to January 1922. Perhaps Henderson intended it as a direct warning to his son?

11)    At the nickelodeons Bushell mentions, the Troubadours' show would often begin straight after the movie.

12)    I once toured the old Fox Theatre in Atlanta, where the crow's nest section remained intact, and was struck by how spitefully petty some of the indignities imposed there were. The white lavatories downstairs, for example, were courteously labelled "Gentlemen" and "Ladies", but those in the crows' nest simply "Men" and "Women".

**Life on the road.**

1) The dates and venues in this chapter and chapter 13 draw heavily on the itinerary presented in Walter Allen's *Hendersonia*, though I've been able to add a few concerts from other sources. Don't take the exact dates as set in stone – both Allen and I had to rely on a degree of approximation there.

2) I've seen suggestions that Johnson took part in a few of the tour's other early gigs too, but no direct evidence of this. He would have been an expensive act to book, so Pace certainly wouldn't have been able to afford him for more than a handful of appearances.

3) Burns had his own troupe who performed a short musical comedy called *Ephraim, You've Got to Go* as part of the evening's variety bill. Bushell credits White with having one of the most beautiful voices he'd ever heard, adding that he sang both blues and opera in his act. One of the two dance duos in the Philadelphia show was Tucker & Gresham and the other Slater & Hollins, but I know nothing about either of them.

4) Philadelphia's Horseshoe Hotel went on to be listed in *The Negro Motorist's Green Book*, a guide to restaurants and accommodation where Black visitors were welcome, and was still included there till the early 1960s. This is the same publication referred to in both *The Green Book* movie and HBO's *Lovecraft Country*.

5) Bushell was born in 1902 and would have just turned 19

when the Philadelphia gig took place. At another stop on the tour, he took offence at something Charlie Jackson, the band's violinist, said to him and "cut a big chunk out of his arm" with a switchblade. "That hurt me because he and I were so close," Bushell writes. "Oh, I was mean then. I had a short temper and was going in the wrong direction."

6) Walton's political career began with a successful 1913 campaign to persuade American newspapers that the word "Negro" should be given an initial capital– just as *The New York Times* decided to do with 'Black" in 2020. It was his experience on the Southern leg of Black Swan's tour in 1922 which convinced him to work full-time on civil rights. He ran publicity for the Democratic National Committee's coloured division in 1924 and was appointed US Minister to Liberia eleven years later.

7) These places were known as buffet flats because they laid out a selection of liquor and cold food for waiting customers. Likely as not, there'd be a female blues singer or pianist keeping people entertained in this anteroom too. Alberta Hunter and many others began their singing careers in just this way.

8) Bushell puts Tally's weight at over 200lbs, adding rather bizarrely that this made her "too big to get in bed with a man". Perhaps that's how she looked to a 19-year-old meeting her for the first time, but I can't imagine Tally let him hold on to that delusion for long.

9) $500 in 1921 would be worth about $7,500 today.

10)    "Bouchard" is an old Louisiana term for anyone with a big mouth.

11)    The band was booked to play Chicago's Grand Theatre for a week from January 16 onwards. Either Bushell figured it would take him that long to catch up with them, or just decided to grab the first train out of Louisville that he could.

12)    I looked up Tiny Tally in the newspaper archive just to check she wasn't a figment of Bushell's imagination. Sure enough, there she is in 1918, charged with running a disorderly house.

13)    The *Chicago Defender* quote here, like the "type of song" one above it, is taken from the paper's May 7, 1921 edition.

14)    I don't know if Pace followed up on his threat to sue Columbia or not. If so, it seems not to have made the papers.

15)    The Troubadours' support acts in Chicago included the

Gus Smith Trio (singers & dancers) and the comedians Gulfport & Brown. Williams was working with a dance partner called Froncell Manley now, performing their "whirlwind dancing speciality".

16)	Johnson later recorded a solo piano number called *Harlem Strut* for Black Swan. It was released with another instrumental on its B side – that one played by Henderson. Berresford & Shor call Henderson's performance "a creditable jazz solo".

17)	Hunter had another run-in with Waters when she joined the cast of the 1939 Broadway show *Mamba's Daughters*, where Waters already had top billing. "She treated me like a dog," Hunter later said. "Fine artist but, oh, she was so mean. I would sing that song at the end, *Time's Drawing Nigh*, and people would come backstage asking for me, not for Ethel. She called me every name in the book and wanted to hit me."

18) Bizarrely, this contest was sponsored by the 15th US Infantry Regiment. Perhaps they saw it as a way of attracting potential recruits?


## Half the band quits.

1) These figures were prominently reported in Black newspapers at the beginning of December 1921, so it's very likely the Troubadours had seen them. My own source, the *Chicago Defender* of December 3, 1921, placed them at the top of its front page with an accompanying editorial.


## Four months of Jim Crow.

1) This ad appeared in the *Daily Ardmoreite* of February 28, 1922.

2) The victim of the Texarkana lynching was a Black man called NP Norman, who died on February 11, 1922. He'd been arrested on minor charges after humiliating the town's deputy sheriff, Will Jordan, then wrongly blamed for the recent murder of a white shopkeeper. Jordan claimed Norman had been taken from his custody by force, and that it was these vigilantes who'd later shot him dead on a country road. A Grand Jury disagreed, and indicted Jordan himself for the murder.

3) The kidnappers' quote here is taken from the *Kansas City Times* of July 27, 1921.

4) Judge PA Turner was speaking at the Grand Jury

investigation into Norman's death. His quote appears in the *Wichita Daily Times* of February 22, 1922.

5) I often wonder how Henderson felt about the privations of this tour. He was used to a more comfortable middle-class existence than the rest of the Troubadours and a few years older too. They were happy to shrug off the lousy accommodation and short rations in return for all the fun they were having, but would that have been true for him too?

6) This broadcast really was ground-breaking stuff. Even Duke Ellington wouldn't get his first radio performance until August 1923.

7) These are an example of the midnight shows Waters mentions in this chapter's opening quote. Several of the tour's larger Southern venues added them for the Troubadours' show, including the one in Savannah.

8) It's sometimes suggested that Armstrong jammed with The Jazz Masters while they were in New Orleans, but I've seen no evidence that's the case.

9) Armstrong seems to have come to much the same conclusion himself. When 1924 brought a second chance to join Henderson's band, he grabbed it with both hands. He'd later reunite with Singleton in the Hot Five.

10)   This wasn't just marketing hype. Manufacturers really did add radium to all sorts of consumer products in the 1920s, and happily boasted of doing so in their ads.

11)   *Wilmington Morning Star,* May 21, 1922.

12)   This *Wilmington Tribune* review is reproduced in the *New York Age* of June 3, 1922.

13)   These prices appeared in a *Greensboro Daily News* ad of May 26, 1922.

14)   A second Black Swan Troubadours tour began in January 1923, this time with the label's Josie Miles as headliner and Arthur Ray leading a new Jazz Masters line-up. Miles had made several discs for Black Swan by that time, the first of which was *Please Don't Tickle Me Babe / When You're Crazy Over Daddy.*

## Passing for coloured.

1) *New York Age*, March 15, 1924.
2) Letter from DuBois to Pace, March 22, 1922.
3) *Dallas Express*, February 11, 1922.
4) *Black Dispatch,* November 2, 1922.
5) *New York Age,* April 29, 1922.

6) The $100,000 figure comes from a *Black Dispatch* story of December 22, 1921.

7) In his 2004 essay, *Co-Workers in the Kingdom of Culture: Black Swan Records and the Political Economy of African-American Music*, David Suisman presents a table showing Black Swan had 10 of the 20 Black artists recording in the second half of 1922, but only eight of the 39 recording six months later.

8) The language used in the white companies' race records catalogues was just as patronising as these images. "Every smilin', teasin' brownskin gal in dis book of Greatest Blues has jes' got it natchely, the dawgone Blues," Okeh's 1924 catalogue declared.

9) *Richmond Planet*, September 23, 1922.

10)     *Dallas Express,* September 23, 1922.

11)     There was a particularly bitter industrial dispute going on between the mine owners and their workers at the time. I've searched the newspaper archive for any sign of police solving the puzzle of who planted the bomb but found nothing.

12)     The influx of white advertising revenue for Black newspapers like the *Chicago Defender* and *New York Age* was an unexpected bonus of the race records boom.

13)     *Crisis*, December 1922.

14)     These slogans peppered Black Swan ads in both *Crisis* and the *Chicago Defender*, as well as appearing on the all the label's record sleeves.

15)     DuBois endorsed this approach in a November 1923 speech at the Pan-African Conference in London. "[He] instanced the manner in which the American phonographic record companies are now trying to oust a negro concern in providing records for the negro population," the *Guardian* reported. "It may be found, he said, that the only way their competition can be met is by appealing for the support of the smaller concern as an 'All Black' one."

16)     Interview with the author, March 2007.

17)     Radio sales figures are sourced from Suisman (above).

18)     In most cases, Pace and Fletcher would simply make these names up. Occasionally, they'd rope in a real name people knew was associated with Black Swan, claiming the white records were by "Ethel Waters' Jazz Masters" (used three times in the renaming programme) or "Henderson's Dance Orchestra" (used six times).

### Pace battles Marcus Garvey.

1) Besides Pace, the letter's signatories were: Robert Abbott (editor of the *Chicago Defender*); Chandler Owen (secretary of the Friends of Negro Freedom); Robert Bagnall (a director of the NAACP); John Nail (a real estate entrepreneur and director of Black Swan); Julia Coleman (president of the Hair-Vim Chemical Company); William Pickens (field secretary, NAACP) and George Harris (New York alderman).

2) Pace may have inherited his dislike of Garvey from his old mentor. In May 1924, DuBois wrote a scorching editorial in *Crisis* calling Garvey "without doubt the most dangerous enemy of the Negro race in America and in the world. He is either a lunatic or a traitor."

3) An octoroon was someone with one-eighth Black blood - one Black great-grandparent in other words. A quadroon had one-quarter Black blood, which is to say one Black grandparent.

### The dying Swan.

1) Letter from Pace to Black Swan shareholders, July 25, 1923.

2) In fact, Waters seems to have recorded for Aeolian even before Pace thought she did. Reconstructed catalogues for Aeolian's Vocalion label show her recording two sides there on June 1, 1923: *Kind Lovin' Blues* and *I Want My Sweet Daddy Now*. I don't know how the two lawsuits over this issue were resolved.

3) Details of the Waters lawsuit appeared in *New York Age* on July 21, 1923.

4) DuBois was as busy as ever and had many other better uses for the cash he had tied up in Pace's enterprises. In October 1923, for example, his priority was raising enough money to cover his mortgage for the three months he'd be away at London's Pan-African Conference.

5) *New York Age*, March 15, 1924.

6) *Crisis*, May 1924.

7) Pace tells Ottley that he also had Black Swan records pressed by a plant in Connecticut for a year or so, but it's not clear whether this was before or after the Paramount deal.

8) Letter from Pace to Black Swan shareholders, October 21, 1925.

### Afterlives.

1) This was an important enough moment to be given a scene in

Goodman's 1956 Hollywood biopic, *The Benny Goodman Story*. Henderson is played by Sammy Davis Jr's dad.

2) *A Pictorial History of Jazz*, by Orrin Keepnews & Bill Grauer Jr (Spring Books, 1960).

3) *The Swing Era*, by Gunther Schuller (Oxford University Press, 1989).

4) My article's available on PlanetSlade.com. Look for the piece called *A Georgia Lynching*.

5) *Broadway: The American Musical*, episode 3 (PBS, 2012).

6) *New York Post*, November 11, 1969.

7) *Chicago Defender,* July 8, 1933.

8) Just as DuBois had been a surrogate father for Pace, Johnson seems to have become his surrogate son.

9) I've cheated slightly here by combining two different Johnson quotes, the first from a video interview he gave to the National Visionary Leadership Project, and the second from his 1989 autobiography *Succeeding Against the Odds.*

## Hansberry v Lee.

1) The house Pace chose was at 413 East 60th Street.

2) Burke's motivation is described in Truman Gibson's book *Knocking Down Barriers: My Fight for Black America* (Northwestern University Press, 2005). Gibson was a member of Dickerson's courtroom team in Hansberry v Lee.

3) Mamie Hansberry's interview appeared in the *Chicago Tribune* of February 10, 2010.

4) Hansberry's unpublished *NYT* letter appears in *To be Young, Gifted and Black: Lorraine Hansberry in her own Words*, ed Robert Nemeroff (Prentice-Hall, 1969).

5) Pace was busy elsewhere too: in August 1938, he cut the ribbon on the first three of 30 new houses Supreme Liberty Life had built in Washington's Clay Place neighbourhood. The purpose of the development, he said, was to provide affordable housing for Black buyers, to employ Black craftsmen in the houses' construction and to give SLL policyholders a sound investment. Similar SLL developments were already under way in Chicago and Greenfield, Ohio.

6) Lorraine Hansberry studied with DuBois in the early 1950s, quickly becoming his favourite pupil, just as Pace had done half a century earlier. She adored the old professor, calling him "freedom's passion, refined and organized," in a 1953 poem.

## Burying a secret.

1) Until 1960, the race designation on each family's census form was filled in by the census taker, sometimes using information about how individuals were perceived in their community or rules based on their share of "black blood". Whether this particular census taker based his verdict on a conversation with Harry or simply on a quick glance at his skin colour, we don't know.

2) It's also worth noting that Pace published a 1934 self-help book called *Beginning Again* but makes no mention of his extraordinary life story anywhere in the book's text. Doing so would have risked revealing he was Black, and it seems that's something he was no longer prepared to do.

3) *Succeeding Against the Odds*, by John Johnson (Warner Books, 1989).

4) *New York Age*, July 31, 1943.

5) It's tempting to speculate that the "prominent Harlemite" was DuBois or Handy, but neither of them quite fit the bill. DuBois began working with Pace on *Moon Illustrated Weekly* in 1904, exactly 39 years before the *NYA* story appeared, but at the time of Pace's death he was living in Atlanta, not Harlem. Handy was still in New York, but he'd first met Pace in 1907, three years too late to fit the *NYA* description.

6) Ethlynde died three years after Harry, at which point Harry Jr and Josephine sold the family's remaining Supreme Liberty Life shares, a move which severed their last connection to the Black community. They both continued to present as white for the rest of their lives and told their own children nothing about their true heritage.

7) The BBC programme we made was called *King Size Papas,* and broadcast for the first time on Radio 4 in September 2007. It still pops up on the iPlayer from time to time.

8) Letter from Susan Pace Hoy to the author, October 2009. Quoted with her permission.

9) Pace Hoy believes that, although her grandfather allowed his children to pass for white, he never did so himself. When I contacted her again in 2021, she asked me to add this footnote to her earlier letter: "Before my Aunt Josephine [Harry's daughter] passed away in 2012, my cousin had given her many news articles, pictures and Wikipedia articles to look at. She was in her nineties at this time. She acknowledged the Wikipedia and news articles, but clearly

couldn't talk about it. She didn't want her daughter to tell her other daughter, Gail, about any of this. My cousin, Lisa, told her that the whole family already knows and how proud we are of her father and our grandfather. It is just so sad that my father and my cousin's mother had to keep this a secret instead of celebrating this great man's life."

*Black Swan Blues*

For more of Paul Slade's writing visit:

# PlanetSlade.com

## Murder Ballads
## Secret London
## and more

"A fantastic website."
– *Dave Henderson, Mojo.*

"Compelling stuff."
– *Ian Anderson, fRoots.*

"One of the best you can find on the web."
– *Peter Watts, Time Out London.*

*Black Swan Blues*

Made in the USA
Coppell, TX
08 October 2021